# PAINTING WITH
# OILS
# ACRYLICS
# & GOUACHE

# PAINTING WITH
# OILS
# ACRYLICS
# & GOUACHE

Learn to build
confidence
and skill
levels with
30 practical
exercises

**IAN SIDAWAY**

**southwater**

This edition is published by Southwater

Southwater is an imprint of Anness Publishing Ltd
Hermes House, 88–89 Blackfriars Road, London SE1 8HA
tel. 020 7401 2077; fax 020 7633 9499
www.southwaterbooks.com; info@anness.com

© Anness Publishing Ltd 2005

UK agent: The Manning Partnership Ltd
6 The Old Dairy, Melcombe Road, Bath BA2 3LR
tel. 01225 478444; fax 01225 478440
sales@manning-partnership.co.uk

UK distributor: Grantham Book Services Ltd
Isaac Newton Way, Alma Park Industrial Estate
Grantham, Lincs NG31 9SD
tel. 01476 541080; fax 01476 541061
orders@gbs.tbs-ltd.co.uk

North American agent/distributor: National Book Network
4501 Forbes Boulevard, Suite 200, Lanham, MD 20706
tel. 301 459 3366; fax 301 429 5746
www.nbnbooks.com

Australian agent/distributor: Pan Macmillan Australia
Level 18, St Martins Tower, 31 Market St, Sydney, NSW 2000
tel. 1300 135 113; fax 1300 135 103
customer.service@macmillan.com.au

New Zealand agent/distributor: David Bateman Ltd
30 Tarndale Grove, Off Bush Road, Albany, Auckland
tel. (09) 415 7664; fax (09) 415 8892

A CIP catalogue record for this book is available from
the British Library.

Publisher: Joanna Lorenz
Editorial Director: Helen Sudell
Editor: Elizabeth Woodland
Consultant Editor: Sarah Hoggett
Photographer: George Taylor
Designer: Nigel Partridge
Jacket Designer: Nigel Partridge
Project Contributors: Abigail Edgar and Ian Sidaway
Editorial Readers: Rosanna Fairhead and Lindsay Zamponi
Production Controller: Claire Rae

Previously published as part of a larger volume,
*The Practical Encyclopedia of Acrylics, Oils and Gouache*

1 3 5 7 9 10 8 6 4 2

## Acknowledgements

Special thanks to the following artists for their demonstrations and step-by-step projects:
Abigail Edgar: pages 28–9, 46–7, 48–9, 52–3, 57–9, 61 (bottom), 62–3, 69–71, 73–5,
80–1, 83 (bottom right), 84–5, 86 (bottom right), 87.
Ian Sidaway: pages 9–18, 26, 27, 31, 32–3, 35, 38–41, 42–5, 50–1, 52, 56, 60, 61 (top),
64–7, 68, 72, 76–9, 82, 83 (top), 86 (top), 88–95.

Thanks to Jon Hibberd for his kind permission to reproduce the following copyright photographs:
pages 61 (bottom left), 83 (bottom left).

# Contents

# Introduction

The aim of this book is to demonstrate the unique qualities of acrylics, oils and gouache and show you how to exploit them to the full. The book begins with an introduction explaining their characteristics and the best way to handle and work with them. It then sets out the equipment available, including the wide range of oil and acrylic additives and varnishes, and what each one is best used for. A suggested basic starter palette for each medium will set you on the right track without spending a fortune on paints. Then there are a host of demonstrations and practice exercises, from underdrawings and simple washes to glazing, scumbling and the thick impasto work that gives oils and acrylics such a rich, tactile texture. Easy to follow, with clear step-by-step photographs and detailed instructions, these demonstrations and exercises will enable you to master all the painting techniques that you are ever likely to need.

# Oil paint

There are two types of traditional oil paint – professional, or artists', quality and the less expensive students' quality. The essential difference is that artists' quality paint uses finely ground, high-quality pigments, which are bound in the best oils and contain very little filler, while students' paints use less expensive pigments and contain greater quantities of filler to bulk out the paint and give it more body. The filler usually consists of *blanc fixe* or aluminium hydrate, both of which are white pigments with a very low tinting strength.

Students' quality paint is often very good and is, in fact, used by students, amateur painters and professionals alike. The range of colours is more limited but still comprehensive, and each tube of paint in the range, irrespective of its colour, costs the same. Artists' quality paint is sold according to the quality and cost of the pigment used to make it. Each colour in the range is given a series number or letter; the higher the number or letter, the more expensive the paint. Various oils are used to bind the paint and make it workable; linseed, poppy and safflower oil are the most common. The choice of oil depends on the characteristics and drying properties of the pigment being mixed.

### Tubes or tubs? ▶

Oil paint is sold in tubes containing anything from 15 to 275ml (1 tbsp to 9fl oz). If you tend to use a large quantity of a particular colour – for toning grounds, for example – you can buy paint in cans containing up to 5 litres (8¾ pints).

## Oil bars

Like "tube" paint, oil bars can be used to draw on to the support and the paint can be thinned and manipulated in exactly the same way as one would use traditional paint. They can be used in conjunction with traditional oil paint but, because of the added wax content, they are not recommended for heavy or extensive underpainting use.

### Drawing with oils ▼

Oil bars consist of paint with added wax and drying agents. The wax stiffens the paint, enabling it to be rolled into what resembles a giant pastel.

## Alkyd oil paints

A synthetic resin, which is made by combining acid and alcohol, is used in the manufacture of alkyd oil paints. The paints are used in exactly the same way as traditional oil paints and can be mixed with all the traditional mediums and thinners.

The range of colours is not as extensive as that for traditional oil paint, but it is wide enough for most purposes. The largest tube size available is 200ml (7fl oz).

Alkyd-based paint dries much faster than oil-based paint. This makes it very useful for underpainting prior to using traditional oils and for work incorporating glazes or thin layers.

However, you should not use alkyd paint over traditional oil paint, as its fast drying time can cause problems with the stability of the oil paint.

## Water-mixable oil paint

One of the most recent developments in paint technology is water-mixable oil paint. Although it sounds like a contradiction in terms, it was conceived so that people who are allergic to mineral and vegetable solvents could still have access to paint with the handling characteristics of traditional oil paint.

Water-mixable oil paint is made using linseed and safflower oils that have been modified to be soluble in water. Once the paint has dried and the oils have oxidized, it is as permanent and stable as conventional oil paint. Some water-mixable paint can also be used with conventional oil paint, although its mixability is gradually compromised the more traditional paint is added. Water-mixable oil paint is available in tube sizes up to 275ml (9fl oz).

# Oil starter palette

| Ultramarine blue | Cerulean blue | Cadmium red | Alizarin crimson |
|---|---|---|---|
| Cadmium lemon yellow | Yellow ochre | Raw umber | Burnt sienna |

Viridian green          Ivory black

The starter palette shown here is based on readily available colours and should cover most eventualities.

**Ultramarine blue:** originally made from lapis lazuli, it is now more commonly made from an artificial and less expensive pigment that is stable in mixes, although it is relatively slow to dry. The synthetic colour is often sold as French ultramarine. Ultramarine blue is a transparent blue. It has good tinting strength and is the classic "warm" blue.

**Cerulean blue:** a "cool", semi-transparent blue. The artificial pigment is mixed with either linseed or poppy oil and dries relatively fast. Phthalocyanine blue is often used in place of cerulean.

**Cadmium red:** made from an artificial mineral pigment, this is the classic "warm" red. Slow to dry but stable, it is opaque and has good tinting strength.

**Alizarin crimson:** a transparent colour with a high tinting strength. Once made from madder root but now produced synthetically, alizarin is a "cool", slow-drying red. The colour can fade when used in light mixes. Quinacridone red is often used as an alternative.

**Cadmium lemon yellow:** made from an artificial mineral, the colour has a relatively high tinting strength and opacity and is slow to dry. Mixed with cadmium red, it makes a deep cadmium yellow or cadmium orange.

**Yellow ochre:** a natural, relatively opaque earth colour with medium tinting strength, yellow ochre dries moderately slowly and mixes well with most colours.

**Raw umber:** a natural pigment with good tinting strength, raw umber is relatively transparent. It mixes well to create a range of browns. It dries quickly, which makes it ideal for underpainting.

**Burnt sienna:** a fast-drying, bright red-brown with good tinting strength, burnt sienna is relatively transparent.

**Viridian green:** a strong, bright, transparent green with high tinting strength. Viridian mixes well with other colours to create a range of greens. It dries relatively slowly.

**Ivory black:** a natural pigment with a slight brown bias. It has good tinting strength but is slow to dry. It creates a range of interesting greens when mixed with yellow.

You will also need a good white.

**Titanium white** (not shown here): a very bright, opaque white that is not prone to yellowing. The pigment is usually bound in safflower oil and so is slow drying.

## Characteristics of oil paint

Oil paint has been the favoured painting medium of artists for many centuries since its development during the early Renaissance. It is a tried and tested material that, given its relatively long drying time, is astonishingly adaptable and versatile. Works created using oil paint possess a depth and richness of colour that is difficult to achieve with any other type of paint.

Oil paint has a reputation for being difficult to use, but nothing could be further from the truth. The secret lies in efficient preparation and good working practice. Because oil paint takes a long time to dry, you can easily rectify mistakes by simply wiping or scraping off the wet paint and repainting. Alternatively, you can paint over the area in question once the first layer of paint is dry. The long drying time,

together with the smooth, creamy consistency of the paint, also allows you to blend colours and tones seamlessly. It also means that expressive brush work and vibrant colour combinations can be achieved by working paint wet into wet. However, this same drying characteristic can lead to areas being overworked, and without discipline can result in jumbled and muddy colours. Unlike fast-drying acrylics, unused paint can be left for a limited time on the palette between painting sessions without the danger of it drying out.

Oil paint can be used thick or thin and mixed with various oils and additives to increase and improve its handling. Paint used straight from the tube is the consistency of toothpaste and unless it is brushed smooth it will hold the brush mark. The paint can

easily be thickened further by mixing in an additive that increases the volume or amount of paint without altering the depth of colour. These types of additives also contain drying agents, without which thick impasto applications of paint might take months, if not years, to harden and dry.

The paint is thinned using thinners or diluents. These can be used alone or mixed with various oils to create painting mediums. Many ready-prepared mediums can be purchased from art stores, including mediums that enable the paint to be thinned and used as transparent glazes. If the smell of white spirit and turpentine is unpleasant, low-odour thinners are available that do the same job as traditional thinners without their associated smell.

## Good working practice

However you use and apply oil paint and whatever techniques you elect to use, the most important rules are to work on correctly prepared supports and always to work "fat over lean".

"Fat" paint, or paint that contains oils, is flexible and slow to dry, while

"lean" paint contains little or no oil, is inflexible and dries quickly. Oil paintings are often painted in layers and can be unstable and prone to cracking if lean (inflexible, quick to dry) paint is placed over fat (flexible, slow to dry) paint. For this reason, any

underpainting and initial blocking in of colour should always be done using paint that has been thinned with a solvent and to which no extra oil has been added. Oil can be added to the paint in increasing amounts in subsequent layers.

**Working "fat over lean"** ▲
The golden rule when using oil paint is to work "fat" (or oily, flexible paint) over "lean", inflexible paint that contains little or no oil.

**Glazing with oils** ▲
Oils are perfect for glazes (transparent applications of paint over another colour). The process is slow, but quick-drying glazing mediums can speed things up.

**Thick and thin paint** ▶
Oil paint can be used straight from the tube (left) or thinned using a medium or solvent (right).

**Working wet into wet** ▼
The slow drying time of oil paint gives you the chance to work at your leisure and blend colours and tones together on the canvas.

**Paint straight from the tube** ▼
Paint applied straight from the tube holds its shape and the mark of the brush. For heavy impasto work, the paint can be thickened further by using an additive.

## Mixing colours with oils

Colour mixing with oils is relatively straightforward, as there is no colour shift as the paint dries: the colour that you apply wet to the canvas will look exactly the same in intensity when it has dried, so (unlike acrylics, gouache or watercolour) you do not need to make allowances for colour changes as you paint. However, colour that looks bright when it is applied sometimes begins to look dull as it dries. This is due to the oil in the paint sinking into a previously applied absorbent layer of paint below. You can revive the colour in sunken patches by "oiling out" – that is, by brushing an oil-and-spirit mixture or applying a little retouching varnish over the affected area.

**No change in colour when dry** ▼
Unlike acrylic and watercolour paints, the depth and intensity of oil colours remains the same even when the paint has dried.

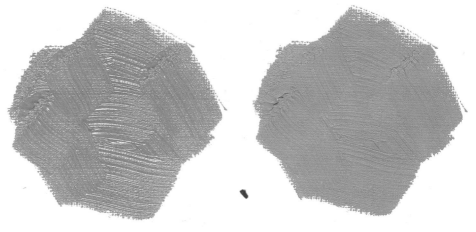

Wet oil paint

Dry oil paint

# Acrylic paint

Perhaps the most important and far-reaching advance in artists' materials in the last 100 years has been the formulation of water-mixable acrylic paint. Acrylic resins were formulated in the 1920s and 1930s, although it took several years before a liquid acrylic emulsion that dried to a clear film was used to carry and bind together pigment. The first commercially available paint based on these emulsions was made available in the 1950s.

Acrylic paint can be mixed with a wide range of acrylic mediums and additives and is thinned with water. Unlike oil paint, it dries quickly and the paint film remains extremely flexible and will not crack. The paint can be used with a wide range of techniques, from thick impasto, as with oil paint, to thin, semi-transparent washes, as with watercolour. Indeed, most if not all of the techniques used in both oil and watercolour painting can be used with acrylic paint. Acrylic paint should not be thought of as an alternative to either, however, but as a very adaptable and unique painting material in its own right.

Acrylic paint is made by suspending pigment in an acrylic emulsion; in some paint formulations, several slightly different emulsions are combined. The paint may also contain various dispersants to ensure the uniform distribution of the pigments, defoamers, preservatives and thickeners.

Both students' and artists' quality acrylic paint is made. As with oil paint, artists' quality paint is available in a wide range of colours, with the cost depending on the pigments used. A less extensive range of colours is available in the students' range and the cost is the same across the whole range.

Acrylic paints come in three different consistencies. Tube paint tends to be of a buttery consistency and holds its shape when squeezed from the tube. Tub paint is thinner and more creamy in consistency, which makes it easier to brush out and cover large areas. There are also liquid acrylic colours that are the consistency of ink and are often sold as acrylic inks.

**Liquid acrylics**
Liquid acrylics are the consistency of ink.

It has been suggested that, because they are made using slightly different formulations, you should not use or mix together paint from different manufacturers. You may experience no problems in mixing different brands or consistencies of paint, but it is always good practice to follow the manufacturers' instructions.

**▲ Tubes and jars**
Acrylic paint is available in tubes and jars of various sizes.

## Characteristics of acrylic paint

The pigments in acrylic paints are bound with an acrylic resin that is water soluble and virtually odour free. Because it is water soluble, the paint is very easy to use, requiring only the addition of clean water. Water is also all that is needed to clean up wet paint after a work session. Once it has dried, however, acrylic paint creates a permanent hard but flexible film that will not fade or crack and is impervious to further applications of acrylic or oil paint and any of their associated mediums or solvents.

Acrylic paint dries relatively quickly: a thin film will be touch dry in a few minutes and even thicker applications dry in a matter of hours. Unlike oil

**Texture gels ▲**
Various gels can be mixed into acrylic paint to give a range of textural effects. These can be worked into while the paint is still wet.

**Mediums and additives ▲**
A wide range of mediums and additives can be mixed into acrylic paint to alter and enhance its handling characteristics.

**Adhesive qualities ▲**
Many acrylic mediums have very good adhesive qualities, making them ideal for collage work.

paints all acrylic colours, depending on the thickness of paint used, dry at the same rate.

Athough hardened paint can be removed with strong paint strippers, this will quickly ruin your brushes. Wet paint, however, can easily be removed by rinsing in water. Try to get into the habit of rinsing your brushes regularly as you work.

Paint can also quickly dry on the palette, although you can avoid this by laying out and mixing only small quantities of paint and by spraying your palette periodically with clean water or using a special "stay-wet" palette.

The unique qualities of acrylic paint mean that many of the techniques that are commonly used with both oil paint and watercolour can be used. Acrylic paint is also excellent when used for underpainting prior to completing a work in oils, but it should not be used over oil paint.

However, it would be a mistake to see acrylic paint as a substitute for any of these traditional materials. It is, in fact, very different from other media and needs to be treated as such. Thinned with water and used on paper, acrylic paint behaves like watercolour paint – the big difference being that once it is dry, acrylic paint is no longer re-soluble. It also behaves like oil paint and can be used thickly, straight from the tube, to build up heavily textured areas of paint. Unlike oil paint, it dries in a matter of minutes – and this can make blending colours together, even over a small area, somewhat difficult.

Manufacturers have thought of many of these problems, and over the years since acrylics were first invented, they have steadily introduced a long list of mediums and additives. Perhaps one of the main advantages of acrylic paint, especially for abstract painters or for artists who like to work on a large scale, is the use of additives that extend or bulk out the amount of paint without altering its handling characteristics or depth of colour. Needless to say, using these extenders in large works makes economic sense, as you can make a relatively small amount of paint go much further.

Acrylic paint and acrylic painting mediums also have good adhesive qualities, which are useful if you are making mixed-media works that include collaged materials.

**Extending drying time** ▲
The drying time of acrylic paint can be extended by using a retarding medium, which gives you longer to work into the paint and blend colours.

**Glazing with acrylics** ▲
Acrylic colours can be glazed by thinning the paint with water, although a better result is achieved by adding an acrylic medium.

**Covering power** ▲
Acrylic paint that is applied straight from the tube has good covering power, even when you apply a light colour over a dark one.

**Shape-holding ability** ▲
Like oil paint, acrylic paint that is applied thickly, straight from the tube, holds its shape and the mark of the brush as it dries.

**Lightening acrylic colours** ▼
Acrylic colours can be made lighter by adding white paint, which maintains opacity (below top), or by adding water, which increases transparency (bottom).

## Acrylics starter palette

Ultramarine blue

Phthalocyanine blue

Cadmium red

Quinacridone red

Cadmium yellow light

Yellow ochre

Raw umber

Burnt umber

Phthalocyanine green

Payne's grey

As always, this range is only a suggestion and can be extended if a particular subject demands it.
**Titanium white** (not shown): this is the only white available in acrylic. It is a bright, opaque white with a high tinting strength.
**Ultramarine blue:** a deep, warm, transparent blue that is permanent and has a high tinting strength.
**Phthalocyanine blue:** a strong, deep, vivid blue available with either a red or a green undertone. Use sparingly, as it has an incredibly high tinting strength.
**Cadmium red:** a warm, opaque red with good tinting strength.
**Quinacridone red:** a very bright red with high tinting strength. Cooler than cadmium red, it makes very good purples when mixed with phthalocyanine blue.

**Cadmium yellow light:** a relatively opaque yellow that mixes well with red to create a range of orange hues and with blue to create a range of intense greens.
**Yellow ochre:** a semi-opaque earth colour with relatively low tinting strength. It is good for modifying other colours.
**Raw umber:** a useful transparent earth colour with low tinting strength.
**Burnt umber:** a rich, deep, warm brown, which is a good starting point for mixing a range of other browns.
**Phthalocyanine green:** a brilliant strong green with a high tinting strength. This is a good "base" from which to mix a wide range of greens.
**Payne's grey:** a transparent blue-grey with relatively low tinting strength that is useful for modifying other colours.

**Change in colour when dry** ▼
One of the fundamental differences between oil and acrylic paint is the slight darkening of colour as acrylic paint dries. This is due to the milky appearance of the wet acrylic emulsion binder: as the emulsion dries it becomes clear and transparent, allowing the pigment it is carrying to be seen more clearly. It can be difficult to judge the exact tone or intensity of your mixes.

Wet acrylic paint    Dry acrylic paint

# Gouache paint

Made using the same pigments and binders found in transparent watercolour, gouache is a water-soluble paint. The addition of *blanc fixe* – a precipitated chalk – gives the paint its opacity. Because gouache is opaque you can paint light colours over darker ones – unlike traditional watercolour, where the paint's inherent transparency means that light colours will not cover any darker shades that lie underneath.

Recently some manufacturers have begun to introduce paint made from acrylic emulsions and starch. The best-quality gouache contains a high proportion of coloured pigment. Artists' gouache tends to be made using permanent pigments that are light fast. The so-called "designers" range of colours uses less permanent pigments, as the work produced by designers is intended to last for only a short time.

Gouache paint is available in tubes and jars. Some brands are sold in series, with the price reflecting the varying cost of the raw materials, while other brands cost the same across the range. Different brands can be mixed, and the range of colours available is relatively wide. Tube and jar colours have much the same consistency.

## What to purchase

Tubes of gouache are large enough for most purposes, although you might like to consider buying a larger jar for colours that you use a lot of, such as permanent white (good for highlights) or zinc white (good for mixing with other colours to lighten them).

All of the equipment and techniques used with watercolour can be used with gouache. Like watercolour, gouache can be painted on white paper or board; due to its opacity and covering power, it can also be used on a coloured or toned ground and over gesso-primed board or canvas. Gouache is typically used on smoother surfaces that might be advised for traditional watercolour, as the texture of the support is less of a creative or aesthetic consideration.

If they are not used, certain gouache colours are prone to drying up over time. Gouache does remain soluble when dry, but dried-up tubes can be a problem to use.

Certain dye-based colours are very strong and, if used beneath other layers of paint, can have a tendency to bleed through. These colours should be avoided or used only in overlying layers.

Gouache paint

## Characteristics of gouache

Gouache paint is water based and remains water-soluble when dry. This allows you to remove paint easily – but it also means that you need to take care when working over previously applied paint layers. If the brushwork is anything but direct and sure, it can pick up previously applied paint, resulting in muddy and confused colour.

Gouache can be used as thin, dilute, semi-transparent washes like watercolour or, due to its innate density, applied to form a thicker, opaque film. As with traditional watercolour, you can

**Work confidently** ▲
Gouache remains soluble when it is dry, so if you are applying one colour over another, your brushwork needs to be confident and direct: a clean, single stroke, as here, will not pick up paint from the first layer.

**Muddied colours** ▲
If you scrub paint over an underlying colour, you will pick up paint from the first layer and muddy the colour of the second layer, as here.

**Blending colours** ▲
Gouache colours can be blended together wet into wet on the support, so that colours merge together almost imperceptibly.

lighten the colour simply by thinning it with water: this increases its transparency and allows more of the support of a previously applied layer of paint to show through. Alternatively, you can add white paint, which increases the opacity and enables you to paint light colours over darker ones.

The paint film shrinks as it dries: if you apply gouache too thickly, therefore, you run the risk of the paint cracking. You can overcome this simply by re-wetting a cracked area: this makes the paint soluble again, allowing you to brush or clean off some paint. Once it is dry, the area can be repainted if required.

Due to the high chalk content of the paint, there is a slight colour shift as the paint dries: gouache generally looks a little lighter when it is dry than it does when it is wet. As with acrylics, it will not take you long to get used to this and to compensate by making your wet mixes slightly stronger or more intense. Always test any mixes on a piece of scrap paper and wait for them to dry before you apply them to your actual painting.

It can sometimes be difficult to obtain dark, deep rich colour with gouache so, although it is often necessary to add white paint to mixtures, this should be done with care.

**Wet into wet** ▲
Like transparent watercolour paint, gouache paint can be worked wet into wet (as here) or wet on dry.

**Removing dry paint** ▲
Dry paint can be re-wetted and removed by blotting with an absorbent paper towel.

### Change in colour when dry
Gouache paint looks slightly darker when dry than it does when wet, so it is good practice to test your mixes on a piece of scrap paper – although, with practice, you will quickly learn to make allowances for this.

Wet gouache paint

Dry gouache paint

**Lightening gouache colours** ▲
Gouache colours can be made lighter either by adding water, which increases transparency (above left), or by adding white paint, which maintains opacity (above right).

## Gouache starter palette

Cadmium red     Quinacridone red     Cadmium yellow light     Yellow ochre

Ultramarine blue     Phthalocyanine blue     Phthalocyanine green     Raw umber

Payne's grey     Burnt umber

The colours suggested here will provide you with a good, multi-purpose palette of gouache paints from which you will be able to mix virtually any colour that you need. However, you may want to adapt or extend the list if you tend to paint a particular type of subject frequently – portraits or figures, for example, or landscapes. The benefit of using a limited palette such as this is that it will force you to mix your colours carefully, learning as you go. Experiment to see what colours you can create – and get into the habit of making a note of any particularly useful mixes, so that you can recreate them easily the next time you need to use them. You will soon begin to see how different colours can be combined to make new ones.

**Cadmium red:** a warm, opaque red with good tinting strength.

**Quinacridone red:** a very bright red with high tinting strength. Cooler than cadmium red, it makes very good purples when mixed with phthalocyanine blue.

**Cadmium yellow light:** a relatively opaque yellow that mixes well with red to create a range of orange hues and with blue to create a range of intense greens.

**Yellow ochre:** a semi-opaque earth colour with relatively low tinting strength. It is good for modifying other colours.

**Ultramarine blue:** a deep, warm, transparent blue that is permanent and has a high tinting strength.

**Phthalocyanine blue:** a strong, deep, vivid blue available with either a red or green undertone. Use it sparingly, as it has an incredibly high tinting strength.

**Phthalocyanine green:** a brilliant strong green with a high tinting strength. This is a good "base" green from which to mix a wide range of other greens.

**Raw umber:** a useful transparent earth colour with low tinting strength.

**Payne's grey:** a transparent blue-grey, with relatively low tinting strength that is useful for modifying other colours.

**Burnt umber:** a rich, deep, warm brown, which is a good starting point for mixing a range of other browns. As with other media, you will also need a white paint in your palette.

**Titanium white (not shown)** is a bright, opaque white with a high tinting strength and is particularly good for painting bright highlights such as sunlight sparkling on water. Zinc white tends to be better for mixing with other colours in order to lighten them.

# Paintbrushes

Brushes are available in a wide range of shapes and sizes, from tiny brushes that consist of just a few hairs or fibres that are used to paint very fine detail to large, flat brushes several inches (centimetres) across. Most brushes are sold in series, with each brush being given a number depending on its size: the higher the number, the larger the brush.

The cost of a brush depends on the quality of the materials from which it is made and on its size. Good-quality brushes are worth their initial high cost as, provided you look after them, they will last longer than cheaper alternatives. Having said that, however, certain types of paint application and painting techniques can be very rough and this, coupled with the corrosive nature of some solvents, means that the bristles or fibres used to make a brush do wear out. In these cases, it can be more economical to use a cheaper alternative.

Regardless of cost, when you are buying brushes discard any that do not hold their shape, lack spring, or have loose fibres or bristles.

## Brush materials

The materials used to make brush fibres may be either natural or synthetic, hard or soft. The type you choose depends on the medium in which you are working.

Oil-painting brushes are traditionally made from bristle from the back of a hog. Today, most bristle is obtained from China, with the best coming from an area known as Chungking. The bristles hold their shape well and the fibres are thick, which means they can hold a substantial amount of paint. In the very best bristle brushes, the end of each bristle is split; this is known as "flagging", and it allows the bristle to hold more paint and distribute it evenly.

Synthetic brushes are good quality and hard wearing. They are also less expensive than either bristle or natural-hair brushes. However, they can quickly lose their shape if they are not looked after and cleaned well. Synthetic brushes can be used with oil, acrylic and gouache.

Natural hair brushes can be made from sable, goat, squirrel, ox and even mongoose hair. Traditionally, natural hair brushes are more often associated with watercolour painting, and so they are ideal for using with gouache. They can also be used with acrylics; in fact, as painting in acrylics draws on techniques that are used in both watercolour and oil painting, it is best to have a selection of hard and soft brushes for acrylics.

There is also a tradition of using sable- and mongoose-hair brushes with oils; the fine-tipped hairs are good for fine detail, although it is not easy to move oil paint around on the canvas with natural-hair brushes. If you do use natural hair brushes with oils or acrylics, however, you must clean them scrupulously after use. Given the availability of good-quality synthetic brushes, it is perhaps better to reserve natural-hair brushes for working in water-soluble media.

## Cleaning brushes

1 Cleaning your brushes thoroughly will make them last longer. Wipe off any excess wet paint on a rag or a piece of newspaper. Take a palette knife and place it as close to the metal ferrule as possible. Working away from the ferrule towards the bristles, scrape off as much paint as you can.

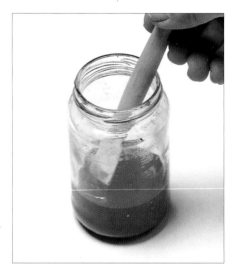

2 Pour a small amount of household white spirit (paint thinner) (or water, if you are using a water-based paint such as acrylic or gouache) into a jar; you will need enough to cover the bristles of the brush. Agitate the brush in the jar, pressing it against the sides to dislodge any dried-on paint.

3 Rub household detergent into the bristles of the brush with your fingers. Rinse the brush thoroughly in clean water until the water runs clear. Reshape the bristles or fibres with your fingertips and store the brush in a jar with the bristles pointing upwards, so that they hold their shape.

# Brush shapes

Several brush shapes are available in bristle, synthetic fibres and natural hair. Although the choice might seem bewildering at first glance, some of the more "specialist" brushes are of limited use, and you would probably do better to experiment with a small range and find out what kind of marks you can make with each one. Finally, do not overlook the range of brushes available from home improvement stores: decorators' brushes can be very useful for laying in large areas of colour – when toning a ground, for example. These are often of a very high quality and cost far less than similar brushes sold in art supply stores.

Regardless of the medium in which you are working, you will need a range of different brush sizes. The shapes that you select are often very much a matter of personal preference, but the following are all useful.

## Flat brushes ▼

These brushes have square ends. They hold a lot of paint, which can be applied as short impasto strokes or brushed out flat. Large flat brushes are useful for blocking in and covering large areas quickly. Short flats, known as "brights", hold less paint and are stiffer. They make precise, short strokes, ideal for impasto work and detail.

## Brushes for fine detail ▶

A rigger brush (top right) is very long and thin. It was originally invented for painting the straight lines of the ropes and rigging on ships in marine painting – hence the rather odd-sounding name. A liner (bottom right) is a flat brush which has the end cut away at an angle. Both of these brushes may be made from natural or synthetic fibres.

## Wash brushes ▶

The wash brush has a wide body, which holds a large quantity of paint. It is used for covering large areas with a uniform or flat wash of paint. There are two types of wash brush: rounded or "mop" brushes (top right), which are commonly used with watercolour and gouache, and flat wash brushes (bottom right), which are more suited for use with oils and acrylics.

## Round brushes ▼

These are round-headed brushes that are used for detail and for single-stroke marks. Larger round brushes hold a lot of paint and are useful for the initial blocking-in. The point on round brushes can quickly disappear, as it becomes worn down by the abrasive action of the rough support. The brushes shown here are made of natural hair.

Rigger brush

Liner brush

Rounded or "mop" brush

Flat wash brush

## Unusually shaped brushes ▼

Fan blenders (below left) are intended for blending together colours on the support. They are also useful for special effects such as drybrush work. A filbert (below right) combines some of the qualities of a flat and a round brush.

Large flat brush

Short flat brush

Large round brush

Small round brush

Fan bender brush

Filbert

# Alternative paint applicators

Although brushes are the most usual means of applying paint to the support, there are a number of other tools that you can use. Some, such as palette and painting knives, are intended specifically for painting, but you can also improvise using virtually anything that comes to hand, including old rags, cardboard and even your fingertips.

## Artist's palette and painting knives

Palette knives are intended for mixing paint with additives on the palette, scraping up unwanted paint from the palette or support, and general cleaning. Palette knives are available with either plastic or stainless steel blades. The steel blades are more durable and can be found in several different shapes. With plastic blades, there is a more limited range of shapes. The blade of most palette knives extends straight out from the wooden handle, although some have a cranked handle. This raises the hand holding the knife clear of the surface being worked on.

Strong knives can also be found in DIY or home improvement stores. Although they are intended for stripping wallpaper or applying quick-drying filler to cracks and holes, they made very good palette knives.

All painting knives have cranked handles. Made from flexible stainless steel, the knives – like brushes – come in different shapes and sizes. You can create a wide range of marks using painting knives. In general, the body of the blade is used to spread paint, the point for detail, and the edge for making crisp linear marks. The knife is not as adaptable as the brush and you will need a range of painting knives in order to create a range of different marks and effects.

Plastic painting knives are also available, but they are not recommended for use with oils or acrylics. They can, however, be used with the more liquid gouache; the gouache seems to be "held" more by the blade, while it is difficult to pick up thin paint using knives with steel blades.

Regardless of the type of knife you use, it is important to clean it thoroughly after use. Paint that has dried on the blade will prevent fresh paint from flowing evenly off the blade. If paint dries on to a steel blade, remove it using paint stripper, the caustic action of which will not damage the blade. Do not use caustic paint strippers on plastic blades, as they will dissolve; instead, peel the paint away. Ideally, you should clean the paint from plastic knives while it is still wet.

**Steel knives**
Painting and palette knives made of steel are available in a range of shapes and sizes. In order to work successfully with this method of paint application, you will require several.

**Plastic knives**
Less expensive and less durable than steel knives, plastic knives manipulate watercolour and gouache paints better than their steel counterparts.

## Paint shapers

A relatively new addition to the artist's range of tools are paint shapers. They closely resemble brushes, but are used to move paint around in a way similar to that used when painting with a knife. Instead of bristle, fibre or hair, the shaper is made of a non-absorbent silicone rubber. Various tip shapes are available in several different sizes and degrees of firmness. They are used in a number of ways to apply and push paint around the support, as well as to remove paint and blend different-coloured areas together. Although they are not as versatile as the brush, they bring a different quality to the work.

Shapers can be used with all types of paint, mediums and adhesives. They are easy to clean, as wet paint can be washed off and dry paint can be peeled off the rubber tip without the use of solvents. Another advantage is that the rubber tip will not harden or wear with use.

## Foam and sponge applicators

Nylon foam is used to make both foam brushes and foam rollers. Both of these are available in a range of sizes and, while they are not intended as substitutes for the brush, they are used to bring a different quality to the marks they make.

Natural sponges have always found a place in the watercolourist's work box and, together with man-made sponges, can be used to good effect with acrylics and gouache. They are invaluable for spreading thin paint over large areas and for making textural marks. They are also useful for mopping up spilt paint and for wiping paint from the support in order to make corrections.

Foam and sponge applicators are better used with water-based mediums than with oil-based ones, as cleaning the applicators first in solvent and then in soap and water can be a long and messy process. With water-based mediums, however, all you need to do is rinse the paint from the applicator by holding it under a running tap.

## Alternative applicators

Paint can be applied and manipulated using almost anything. Artists are, by and large, thoughtful and inventive people, and the only limitations are set by practicality and imagination. The cutlery drawer and tool box are perhaps a good starting point, but you will no doubt discover plenty of other items around the home that you can use. Cardboard, pieces of rag, wood, wire wool and many other seemingly unlikely objects can all be – quite literally – pressed into service.

### Sponge applicators and paint shapers ▼
Shapers (below left) can be used to apply paint and create textures, and to remove wet paint. Foam rollers (below centre) are useful for covering large areas quickly. Sponge applicators (below right) are useful for initial blocking in.

### Natural and synthetic sponges ▼
With their pleasing irregular texture, natural sponges (below top) are used to apply washes and textures. They are especially useful to landscape artists. Synthetic sponges (below bottom) can be cut to the desired shape and size and used in a similar fashion.

### Everyday household items ▼
Although they might not seem like the obvious choice, everyday household items, such as an old rag, wire wool and piece of cardboard shown here, can also be used to apply paint to a support.

Natural sponge

Sponge applicator

Foam roller

Paint shaper

Synthetic sponge

Wire wool

Rag

Cardboard

# Palettes

The surface on which an artist arranges colours prior to mixing them and applying them to the support is known as the palette. Somewhat confusingly, the same word is also used to describe the range of colours used by a particular artist, or the range of colours found in a particular painting. The type of palette that you use depends on the medium in which you are working, but you will undoubtedly find that you need more space for mixing colours than you might imagine. A small palette gets filled with colour mixes very quickly and it is a false economy to clean the mixing area too often: you may be cleaning away not only usable paint, but also mixed colours that you might want to use again. Always buy the largest palette practical.

## Wooden palettes

Flat wooden palettes in the traditional kidney or rectangular shapes with a thumb hole are intended for use with oil paints. They are made from hardwood, or from the more economical plywood.

Before you use a wooden palette with oil paint for the first time, rub linseed oil into the surface of both sides. Allow it to permeate the surface. This will prevent oil from the paint from being absorbed into the surface of the palette and will make it easier to clean. Reapply linseed oil periodically and a good wooden palette will last for ever.

Wooden palettes are not recommended for acrylic paint, as hardened acrylic paint can be difficult to remove from the surface.

**Holding and using the palette** ▼
Place your thumb through the thumb hole and balance the palette on your arm. Arrange pure colour around the edge. Position the dipper(s) at a convenient point, leaving the centre of the palette free for mixing colours.

## White palettes

Plastic palettes are uniformly white. They are made in both the traditional flat kidney and rectangular shapes. The surface is impervious, which makes them ideal for use with either oil or acrylic paint. They are easy to clean, but the surface can become stained after using very strong colours such as viridian or phthalocyanine blue.

There are also plastic palettes with wells and recesses, intended for use with watercolour and gouache. The choice of shape is entirely subjective, but it should be of a reasonable size.

White porcelain palettes offer limited space for mixing. Intended for use with watercolour and gouache, they are aesthetically pleasing but can easily be chipped and broken.

**Wooden palette** ▲
These wooden palettes are generally used for oils. Always buy one that is large enough to hold all the paint and mixes that you intend to use.

**Slanted-well palette** ▲
This type of porcelain palette is used for mixing gouache or watercolour. The individual colours are placed in the round wells and mixed in the rectangular sections.

## Disposable palettes

A relatively recent innovation is the disposable paper palette, which can be used with both oils and acrylics. These come in a block and are made from an impervious parchment-like paper. A thumb hole punched through the block enables it to be held in the same way as a traditional palette; alternatively, it can be placed flat on a surface. Once the work is finished, the used sheet is torn off and thrown away.

**Paper palette** ▲
Disposable palettes are convenient and make cleaning up after a painting session an easy task.

## Stay-wet palette

Intended for use with acrylic paints, the stay-wet palette will stop paints from drying out and becoming unworkable if left exposed to the air for any length of time. The palette consists of a shallow, recessed tray into which a water-impregnated membrane is placed. The paint is placed and mixed on this membrane, which prevents the paint from drying out. If you want to leave a painting halfway through and come back to it later, you can place a plastic cover over the tray, sealing the moist paint in the palette. This prevents the water from evaporating and the paint from becoming hard and unusable. The entire palette can be stored in a cool place or even in the refrigerator. If the membrane does dry out, simply re-wet it.

**Stay-wet palette** ▶
This type of palette, in which the paint is mixed on a water-impregnated membrane, prevents acrylic paint from drying out. If you like, you can simply spray acrylic paint with water to keep it moist while you work.

## Containers for water, solvents and oil

Although a regular supply of containers such as empty jam jars, can be recycled from household waste, several types of specially designed containers are available from art supply stores.

Among the most useful are dippers – small, open containers for oil and solvent that clip on to the edge of the traditional palette. Some have screw or clip-on lids to prevent the solvent from evaporating when it is not in use. You can buy both single and double dippers, like the one shown on the right.

**Dipper** ▼
Used in oil painting, dippers are clipped on to the side of the palette and contain small amounts of oil or medium and thinner.

## Improvised palettes

For work in the studio, any number of impermeable surfaces and containers can be used as palettes. Perhaps the most adaptable is a sheet of thick counter glass, which you can buy from a glazier; the glass should be at least 5mm/¼in thick and the edges should be polished smooth. Glass is easy to clean and any type of paint can be mixed on it. To see if your colours will work on the support you have chosen to use, slip a sheet of paper the same colour as the support beneath the glass.

Aluminium-foil food containers, tin cans, glass jars, paper and polystyrene cups also make useful and inexpensive containers for mixing large quantities of paint and for holding water or solvents. Take care not to put oil solvents in plastic or polystyrene containers, as the containers may dissolve.

# Oil additives

Although oil paint can be used straight from the tube, it is usual to alter the paint's consistency by adding a mixture of oil or thinner (solvent). Simply transfer the oil or thinner to the palette a little at a time and mix it with the paint. Most oil painters attach dippers to the edge of the palette so that the oil and thinner are readily at hand, but any small container will do. There are a great many oils and thinners on the market. Some of the more common ones are shown below.

## Oils and mediums

Oils and mediums are used to alter the consistency of the paint, allowing it to be brushed out smoothly to increase its transparency or to make it dry more quickly. Once exposed to air, the oils dry by oxidization, leaving behind a tough, leathery film that contains the pigment. Different oils dry at a different rate. Because some oils (linseed, for example, which dries relatively quickly) tend to yellow slightly with age, they are used only in the manufacture of darker colours. Delicate colours and white are often manufactured using safflower or poppy oil, both of which dry more slowly. Many oils are made from plant extracts, but more recent additions are made from synthetic resins that also speed up drying.

A painting medium is simply a ready-mixed painting solution that may contain various oils, waxes and drying agents. The oils available are simply used as a self-mixed medium. Your choice of oil or medium will depend on several factors, including cost, the type of finish required, the thickness of the paint being used, and the range of colours.

All oils take several days to dry. The exact drying time, however, depends on the amount used and on atmospheric temperature and humidity.

There are several alkyd-based mediums on the market. They all accelerate the drying time of the paint. Some alkyd mediums are thixotropic; this means that they are initially stiff and gel-like but, once worked, they become clear and loose. Other alkyd mediums contain inert silica and add body to the paint, which is useful for impasto techniques where a thicker mix of paint is required.

## Oils and thinners

There are a great many oils and thinners on the market. The more common ones are listed below.

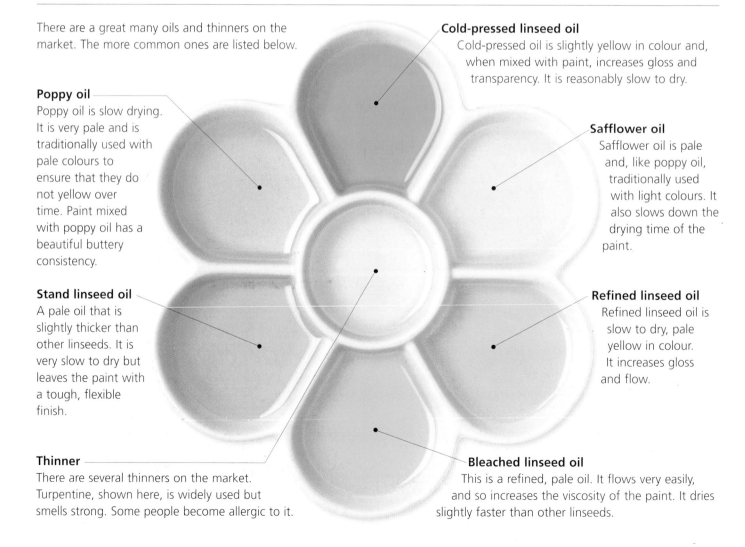

**Cold-pressed linseed oil**
Cold-pressed oil is slightly yellow in colour and, when mixed with paint, increases gloss and transparency. It is reasonably slow to dry.

**Poppy oil**
Poppy oil is slow drying. It is very pale and is traditionally used with pale colours to ensure that they do not yellow over time. Paint mixed with poppy oil has a beautiful buttery consistency.

**Safflower oil**
Safflower oil is pale and, like poppy oil, traditionally used with light colours. It also slows down the drying time of the paint.

**Stand linseed oil**
A pale oil that is slightly thicker than other linseeds. It is very slow to dry but leaves the paint with a tough, flexible finish.

**Refined linseed oil**
Refined linseed oil is slow to dry, pale yellow in colour. It increases gloss and flow.

**Thinner**
There are several thinners on the market. Turpentine, shown here, is widely used but smells strong. Some people become allergic to it.

**Bleached linseed oil**
This is a refined, pale oil. It flows very easily, and so increases the viscosity of the paint. It dries slightly faster than other linseeds.

# Thinners

If you dilute oil paints using only oil, the paint may wrinkle or take too long too dry. As the name suggests, a thinner (also known as a diluent) thins the paint, making it easier to brush out. It does not remain in the paint, but evaporates from the surface.

The amount of thinner that you use depends on how loose or fluid you want the paint to be. Do not use too much, however, or you may find that the paint film becomes weak and prone to cracking.

Ideally, any thinner that you use should be clear and should evaporate easily from the surface of the painting without leaving any residue. There are several thinners suitable for use with oil paints. There is very little, if any, difference in appearance between them – but they do have different characteristics.

## Turpentine

Distilled from the thick, resinous sap or oleoresin of several different species of pine tree, turpentine is colourless, with a distinct odour. Many people develop an allergy to it, so use it with care and make sure that the room in which you are working is well ventilated.

Turpentine is the strongest and best of all the various thinners used in oil painting. Use only fresh turpentine, as old turpentine can become discoloured with a gummy residue if it is exposed to air and light. To minimize the risk of this happening, store your turpentine in closed metal cans or dark glass bottles.

Good-quality turpentine is expensive, so use it only for painting; for cleaning your brushes, use cheaper white spirit.

## White spirit

Paint thinner or white spirit, which is also known as mineral spirit, is a petroleum by-product. It is clear, has a less pronounced smell than turpentine, does not deteriorate over time and dries faster than turpentine. It is inexpensive and can therefore be used both for painting and for cleaning brushes, although ideally it is best used for cleaning brushes. However, it is not as strong a solvent as turpentine and can leave the paint surface matt.

## Oil of spike lavender

This exotic-sounding solvent is made from lavender oil and smells wonderful. Unlike other solvents, which speed up the drying time of oil paint, oil of spike lavender slows the drying time. It is very expensive. Like turpentine and white spirit, it is colourless.

## Low-odour thinners

For those who dislike the smell of traditional thinners, are allergic to them, or are simply concerned about the health implications of breathing in the fumes, various low-odour thinners such as sansador have come on to the market in recent years and are now a popular choice. However, the drawback of low-odour thinners is that they are relatively expensive and dry slowly.

## Citrus solvents

You may be able to find citrus thinners. They are thicker than turpentine or white spirit but, like spike lavender oil, smell wonderful. They are more expensive than traditional thinners and slow to evaporate.

## Liquin ▼

Liquin is just one of a number of alkyd painting mediums that speed up drying time considerably – often to just a few hours. It also improves flow and increases the flexibility of the paint film. It is excellent for use in glazes.

## Warning
• Always follow any instructions and warning advice carried on containers.
• All solvents are flammable and should be used in a well-ventilated environment, away from naked flames.
• Avoid contact with the skin and eyes and avoid breathing the fumes.
• Do not use solvents when handling food and drink.
• If you experience any adverse effects when using solvents, switch to a low-odour variety.
• All oil-painting mediums and varnishes can be an irritant and should be used following the same procedures as for solvents.
• Keep a suitable empty container available into which you can pour used solvent. When the container is full, dispose of it at your local refuse or waste disposal centre.

# Acrylic additives

Although acrylic paint can be used straight from the tube or jar, or thinned with water, manufacturers have steadily introduced a wide range of mediums and additives that enable the real potential of the paint to be exploited to its maximum. Scour the shelves of any good art supply store and you will find additives that make the paint finish gloss or matt, thick or thin, textured or smooth.

There are additives that slow down the drying time of the paint, giving you longer to work into it. There are even additives that make colours glow in the dark or turn acrylic into a fabric paint that can withstand being put through a washing machine. The chances are that if you want to do something creative with acrylic paint, there is an additive to enable you to do it.

## Types of finish

Acrylic paints dry to leave a matt or slightly glossy surface. The finish depends entirely on the brand being used. Gloss or matt mediums can be added to leave the surface with the desired finish. Gloss and matt mediums can also be mixed together to give the dry paint varying degrees of sheen. The choice is a personal one. As a general rule, colours on a gloss surface tend to look brighter. It is also preferable to use gloss mediums when glazing colours.

### Gloss and matt mediums ▼
It is impossible to tell simply by looking at it whether a medium will give a matt or a gloss finish. Both gloss (below) and matt (bottom) mediums are relatively thin white liquids that dry clear if applied to a support without being mixed with paint.

**The effect of gloss medium** ▲
Adding gloss medium to the paint increases its transparency. This allows you to build up several thin glazes relatively quickly, leaving the dry paint with a slight gloss sheen. Gloss medium also enhances the depth of colour, improves adhesion to the support and increases the flexibility of the paint. It can be used as an adhesive for collage work. Some manufacturers also advise using gloss medium as a varnish.

**The effect of matt medium** ▲
Matt medium also increases transparency and can be used to make matt glazes. Matt medium has good adhesive properties. It can be thinned with water and used to size canvas, or diluted 50:50 with water and used as a fixative for drawings. Matt mediums are not generally used as varnish, as they can deaden colour and look slightly cloudy.

## Adding flow-improving mediums

Flow-improving mediums reduce the water tension, increasing the flow of the paint and its absorption into the surface of the support.

One of the most useful applications for flow-improving medium is to add a few drops to very thin paint, which can tend to puddle rather than brush out evenly across the surface of the support. This is ideal when you want to tone the ground with a thin layer of acrylic before you begin painting.

When flow-improving medium is used with slightly thicker paint, a level surface will result, with little or no evidence of brushstrokes.

The medium can also be mixed with paint that is to be sprayed, as it assists the flow of paint and helps to prevent blockages within the spraying mechanism.

**Without flow-improving medium** ▲
Very thin acrylic paint tends to puddle rather than brush out evenly.

**Flow-improving medium** ▲
This medium is a colourless liquid and therefore does not affect the colour of the paint.

**With flow-improving medium** ▲
Adding flow-improving medium to thicker paint results in a level surface in which no brushstrokes can be seen.

## Adding retarding mediums

Acrylic paints dry quickly. Although this is generally considered to be an advantage, there are occasions when you might want to take your time over a particular technique or a specific area of a painting – when you are blending colours together or working wet paint into wet, for example. Adding a little retarding medium slows down the drying time of the paint considerably, keeping it workable for longer.

Always follow the manufacturer's instructions regarding how much medium to add to your mixes. Beware of adding too much medium as this can result in the paint becoming sticky and leaving a soft, easily damaged paint film.

**Retarding medium** ▶
Retarding mediums are available as gels (shown here) and as fluids.

## Adding gel mediums

Gel mediums are the same consistency as tube colour. Available as matt or gloss finishes, they are added to the paint in the same way as fluid mediums. They increase the brilliance and transparency of the paint, while maintaining its thicker consistency. Gel medium is an excellent adhesive and extends drying time. Gel mediums can be mixed with various textural substances such as sand or sawdust to create textural effects.

There are also thicker versions of gel mediums, which (not surprisingly) are known as heavy gel mediums. They hold brush or knife marks well, making them ideal for impasto work. Another effect of heavy gel mediums is to extend the working time of the paint. Some brands dry to a translucent finish and others to an opaque one.

Heavy gel mediums have very good adhesive properties and can be mixed with sand or sawdust. It is better to build up very thick applications in several thin layers than in one thick one, as this reduces the chance of any splitting in the paint film due to water evaporation and shrinkage. Very thick applications can be heavy and are best made on non-flexible surfaces such as board, rather than on canvas, which may sag.

**Heavy gel medium** ▲
Heavy gel medium is a thick paste.

◀ **The effect of heavy gel medium**
Mixed with acrylic paint, heavy gel medium forms a thick paint that is used for impasto work.

## Adding modelling paste

Modelling pastes can be mixed with acrylic paint and dry to give a hard finish, which can be sanded or carved into using a sharp knife. They are best used on non-flexible substrates, as thick applications can be heavy, although there is a modelling paste with a lighter structure, which is ideal for use on canvas. If you are using modelling pastes on flexible supports, add a gel medium to maximize flexibility.

In order to aid drying, it is better to build up several thin coats, allowing each layer to dry before adding the next, rather than apply one thick layer. Although heavy applications may crack, they do not affect the structural strength of the application and any cracks can be filled using more paste once the area is dry.

**Modelling paste** ▼
White or light grey in colour, modelling pastes are either smooth to the touch or very slightly granular in texture. As with other acrylic mediums, there are several reputable brands on the market.

**The effect of modelling paste** ▲
Modelling pastes dry to give a hard finish, which can be sanded or carved into using a sharp knife.

# Adding texture pastes and gels

While sand, gravel, sawdust and various other materials can be added to texture paste and other acrylic gel mediums, there are several proprietary texture gels with different textural characteristics. These pastes have fine, medium or coarse textures and resemble sand, stucco, plaster, lava, flakes or fibres. Paint can be mixed into the paste, or the paste can be applied and painted over when dry. To avoid damaging your brushes, it is best to apply texture paste with a knife.

**Natural sand texture gel** ▲
The natural sand texture gel shown here is fine in texture.

**Glass beads texture gel** ▲
Glass beads are embedded in the gel. It looks grainy, like medium-textured sand.

**Black lava texture gel** ▲
Black lava texture gel is speckled grey in appearance.

**Natural sand texture gel** ▲
This gel creates the texture of sand. The colour is more even than real sand.

**Glass beads texture gel** ▲
Glass beads texture gel creates an effect like medium-textured sand.

**Black lava texture gel** ▲
Mixed with a pale colour, as here, the colour of the gel remains visible.

# Pearlescent, iridescent and phosphorescent mediums

These mediums are intended primarily for decorative works. Pearlescent mediums create a shimmering effect. Iridescent mediums contain tiny flakes of mica that, when mixed with paint, appear to change colour depending on the direction of the light. The mediums are particularly effective with transparent colours. Phosphorescent medium is green and glows in the dark. It can be mixed with other colours but the glow effect is gradually reduced.

**The effect of iridescent medium** ▶
Tiny flakes of mica in the medium appear to change colour.

**Iridescent medium** ▲
Iridescent medium looks very similar to some of the other acrylic additives.

# Supports

A "support" is the name for the surface on which a painting is made. It needs to be physically stable and resistant to deterioration from both the corrosive nature of any of the materials being used and the surrounding atmosphere. It needs to be light enough to be transported from one place to another. It also needs to have a sympathetic surface texture, as this will have a direct effect on the marks and techniques that you use. Your choice of support depends on the medium in which you are working.

## Canvas

Without doubt, canvas is the most widely used support for both oil and acrylic work. Several types of canvas are available, made from different fibres. The most common are made from either cotton or linen, both of which can be purchased ready stretched and primed to a range of standard sizes (although there are suppliers who will prepare supports to any size) or on the roll by the metre (yard) either primed or unprimed. Unprimed canvas is easier to stretch.

Linen canvas is made from the fibres of the flax plant, *Linum usitatissimum*. The seeds of this plant are also pressed to make linseed oil, used by artists. Linen is the finest type of canvas available. It is light brown in colour, very strong, and gives a pleasingly receptive surface on which to work. Depending on the gauge or weight of the thread used, linen canvas can be found in a wide variety of weave textures and weights. Linen canvas is often described as being fine, medium or coarse. As a general rule, lighter weights (200–225g/ 7–8oz) with a fine tooth are used for smaller works, while heavier grades (375–450g/12–15oz) are best for larger works. Because of the way linen is woven, the surface texture never looks too even or mechanical.

Cotton canvas is known as cotton duck. It is light cream in colour and has a more regular or mechanical weave than linen. Stretched cotton duck is more stable than linen and is less prone to becoming slack on its stretcher if the air becomes damp. Seen as inferior to linen, it is nonetheless a popular and widely used support. It is substantially cheaper than linen and is also easier to stretch. Cotton duck is available in a range of weights from 200–450g/ 7–15oz; for larger works, use weights over 250g/10oz.

**Linen canvas** ▲
Linen canvas is available in a number of different textures and weights, from very fine to coarse. The fibres are stronger than cotton fibres, which means that the fabric is less likely to sag and stretch over time.

**Cotton duck** ▶
Cotton duck has a more regular (some people might say more mechanical) weave than linen. It is also less expensive than linen.

# Stretching canvas

Canvas must be stretched taut over a rectangular wooden frame before use. For this you will need stretcher bars and wooden wedges.

Stretcher bars are usually made of pine and are sold in pairs of various standard lengths. They are pre-mitred and each end has a slot-in tenon joint. Longer bars are morticed to receive a cross bar (recommended for large supports of 75 x 100cm/30 x 40in or more).

The wooden wedges are tapped lightly into the inside of each corner and can be hammered in further to allow you to increase the tension of the stretched canvas a little if necessary.

1 Press or tap the stretcher bars together to make a frame. They should slot together easily, without you having to exert much pressure.

2 Using a tape measure or piece of string, measure diagonally from corner to corner in both directions to check that the corners are square.

3 Arrange the canvas flat on a work surface. Place the frame on top, bevelled side down. Cut out allowing an overlap of approximately the width of the stretcher bars on all sides.

4 Fold the excess canvas over the stretcher bars, ensuring the canvas threads run parallel to the bars. Drive a staple into the centre of opposite sides. Repeat on the other sides.

5 Insert one staple to each side of the centre staple on opposite sides, half way between the centre staple and the edge. Repeat on the other sides. Fold in the canvas corner and hold in position.

6 Fold over the flap of canvas on one side of the corner, pull it taut and hold it firmly in position with your fingertip.

7 Fold over the remaining flap of canvas and secure with a staple to make a neat mitre, keeping your finger well away from the staple gun.

8 In each corner, push two wedges into the slots in the stretcher bars. If the canvas sags, the wedges can be pushed in further to keep the canvas taut.

## Priming canvas

Canvas is usually sized and primed (or, increasingly, just primed) prior to being worked on. This serves two purposes. The process not only tensions the fabric over the stretcher bars but also (and more importantly in the case of supports used for oil) seals and protects the fabric from the corrosive agents present in the paint and solvents. Priming also provides a smooth, clean surface on which to work.

In traditional preparation, the canvas is given a coat of glue size. The most widely used size is made from animal skin and bones and is known as rabbit-skin glue. It is available as dried granules or small slabs. When mixed with hot water the dried glue melts; the resulting liquid is brushed over the canvas to seal it.

Increasingly, acrylic emulsions are used to size canvas. Unlike rabbit-skin glue, the emulsions do not have to be heated but are used diluted with water.

The traditional partner to glue size is an oil-based primer. Lead white, which is toxic, together with titanium white and flake white, are all used in oil-based primers. In order to penetrate the fibres of the canvas, it should be the consistency of single cream; dilute it with white spirit if necessary.

Traditional primer can take several days to dry, however; a modern alternative is an alkyd primer, which dries in a couple of hours.

Primers based on acrylic emulsion are easier to use. These are often known as acrylic gesso, although they are unlike traditional gesso. Acrylic primer should not be used over glue size, but it can be brushed directly on to the canvas. Acrylic primers can be used with both oil and acrylic paint, but oil primers should not be used with acrylic paints.

Primer can be applied with either a brush or a large palette knife. If a brush is used the weave of the canvas tends to be more apparent.

If you want to work on a toned ground, add a small amount of colour to the primer before you apply it. Add oil colour to oil primer and acrylic colour to acrylic primer.

## Boards

Several types of wooden board make good supports for both oil and acrylic work. The boards can simply be primed with an acrylic gesso, or canvas can be glued to the surface; a technique known as marouflaging. There are three types of board in common use: plywood, hardboard (masonite) and medium-density fibreboard (MDF).

Plywood is made from several thin layers of wood or veneers glued together to form a rigid sheet. The surface veneers are usually made from hardwood and are smooth.

Hardboard is made from exploded wood fibre and is available both tempered and untempered. Tempering with oils or resins makes it harder and more water resistant. Use the softer-surfaced, untempered board, as the hard and somewhat oily surface of tempered board can resist paint. Some hardboards have a rough and a smooth side; you can paint on either side, depending on the effect you want.

MDF, made from compacted wood fibres, is perhaps the best board to use as it is stable and warp resistant. Both sides of MDF are hard and smooth.

All these boards can be found in a range of sizes. If used at a size where they begin to bend, mount rigid wooden battens on the reverse to reinforce them.

## Priming board

Wood was traditionally sized with rabbit-skin glue and then primed with a thixotropic primer in the same way as canvas; nowadays, most artists use ready-made acrylic primer or acrylic gesso primer, which obviates the need for sizing. Acrylic primer also dries much more quickly.

Before you prime your boards, make sure they are smooth and free of dust. You should also wipe over them with methylated spirits to remove all traces of grease.

**1** Using a wide, flat brush or a decorator's brush, apply primer over the board with smooth, vertical strokes. For a very large surface, apply the primer with a paint roller. Allow to dry.

**2** Rub the surface of the board with fine-grade sandpaper to smooth out any ridges in the paint. Blow or dust off any powder.

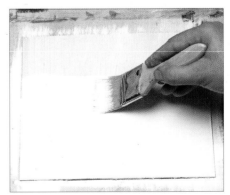

**3** Apply another coat of primer, making smooth horizontal strokes. Allow to dry. Repeat as many times as you wish, sanding between coats.

# Covering board with canvas

Canvas-covered board is a lightweight painting surface that is particularly useful when you are painting on location. Covering board with canvas gives you a support that combines the strength and low cost of board with the texture of canvas. You can use linen or cotton duck, which makes it a good way of using up remnants of canvas; calico, which is a cheap material, is also suitable. Acrylic primer is used to stick the canvas to the board. It looks white when it is first applied, but dries clear. When you have stuck the canvas on to the board, you should leave it to dry for an hour or two in a warm room. Prime the canvas with an acrylic primer before use.

1 Arrange the canvas on a flat surface. Place the board on the canvas. Allowing a 5cm/2in overlap all around, cut out the canvas with a pair of sharp scissors.

2 Remove the canvas from the work surface. Using a wide, flat brush or a household decorator's brush, liberally brush matt acrylic medium over the surface of the board.

3 Place the canvas on the sticky side of the board and smooth it out with your fingertips, working from the centre outwards.

4 Brush acrylic medium over the canvas to make sure that it is firmly stuck down. Place the board canvas-side down on an upturned plate or bowl so that it does not stick to your work surface. Brush acrylic medium around the edges of the board. Fold over the excess canvas, mitring the corners, and brush more medium over the corners to stick them down firmly.

## Canvas paper and board

Artists' canvas boards are made by laminating canvas – or paper textured to look like canvas – on to cardboard. They are made in several sizes and textures and are ideal for use when painting on location. However, take care not to get them wet, as the cardboard backing will disintegrate. They can also be easily damaged if you drop them on their corners. They are ready sized and can be used for both oils and acrylics.

Oil and acrylic papers are also available. Both have a texture similar to canvas and can be bought as loose sheets or as sheets bound together in blocks. Although they are perhaps not suitable for work that is intended to last, they are perfect for sketching and making colour notes.

**Oil and acrylic papers** ▶
Oil and acrylic papers have a texture similar to canvas.

## Paper and illustration board

Although best suited to works using water-based materials, paper and illustration board, provided they are primed with acrylic primer, can also be used for painting in oils.

Watercolour papers provide ideal surfaces for gouache work. The papers are found in various thicknesses and with three distinct surfaces – rough, hot pressed (which is smooth) and NOT or cold pressed, which has a slight texture. Watercolour boards tend to have either a rough or a hot-pressed surface. Illustration board tends to be very smooth and is intended for use with gouache and linework.

**Illustration board** ▶
Used with gouache, illustration board is very smooth and good for finely detailed work.

# Varnishes

Traditionally, varnish was applied to oil paintings to protect them from atmospheric pollution and dirt. Varnish also had an aesthetic purpose: oil painting techniques often result in a paint surface that looks uneven, with dull and shiny areas depending on the amount or type of painting media used. A varnish unifies and enhances the colour, bringing the whole painted surface together beneath a uniform gloss or semi-matt sheen.

The painting must be completely dry before it is varnished, otherwise the drying paint will contract beneath the less flexible varnish and cause the varnish to crack. Oil paintings can take months or even years to dry, depending on the thickness of the paint. Acrylic paintings can be safely varnished with acrylic varnish after a few hours. Watercolours and gouache paintings are normally framed behind glass, so they are protected and there is no need to varnish them.

All varnishes should be flexible. They should remain clear and non-yellowing and be easily removable. Varnishes are made from both natural and synthetic materials. The two traditional natural varnishes are damar and mastic. However, mastic varnish has a reputation for going dark and yellowing with age. It also tends to become cloudy, if it is prepared in damp air, leaving behind a surface bloom.

Varnishes made from natural resins are being replaced by synthetic varnishes made from Ketone and acrylic resins. Synthetic-resin varnishes have several advantages, as they do not yellow with age or become brittle. They can be used on both oil and acrylic paintings. They are also very tough. However, you cannot mix synthetic resin varnishes with oil mediums or turpentine. Several manufacturers market a range of these resins. They are manufactured to dry to a gloss or a matt finish and can be mixed together to provide varnish with varying degrees of sheen.

There are also spray varnishes, both removable and non-removable, which dry to give gloss, satin or matt finishes. They can be used on both oil and acrylic paintings. They are quick drying, but need to be used with care in order to achieve uniform coverage.

## Applying varnish

Make sure the painting is completely dry before you varnish it. Always use a clean varnish brush and work in a dust-free environment.

### The technique ▼
Place your painting flat on a surface. Dip a large, flat brush in your chosen varnish and apply it in smooth, even strokes in one direction. Do not scrub the surface or you will create air bubbles. If you go over any area more than once the finish will be uneven.

## Different types of varnish

Varnishes are pale or colourless and it is difficult to tell the difference between the types by their appearance. Here are some of the most widely used.

### Acrylic matt varnish
Synthetic varnishes can be used on oil and acrylic paintings. The one shown here dries to a matt finish.

### Wax varnish
Wax varnish is used on oil paintings. It is made from beeswax mixed with a solvent. The wax is brushed over the work and allowed to stand for a short time. The excess is then removed with a rag and the surface buffed. The more the surface is buffed, the higher the resulting sheen.

### Acrylic gloss varnish
This synthetic varnish dries to a gloss finish.

### Retouching varnish
Retouching varnish is used on oil paintings and can be used at any time while the work is in progress. It is used to revive sunken areas where the paint looks dull. Both damar and mastic thinned with solvent can be used as retouching varnish.

### Damar varnish
Damar varnish is used on oil paintings. It is made from the resin of the damar tree, which is found throughout Indonesia and Malaysia. The resin is mixed with turpentine to create a slightly cloudy liquid. The cloudiness is caused by natural waxes in the resin, and clears as the varnish dries. Damar does yellow with age, but it is easy to remove it and replace it with a fresh coat. The varnish dries very quickly.

# Auxiliary equipment

Art stores are like candy stores, with shelves full of handsome-looking, colourful materials and equipment. Despite what the manufacturers' catalogues would have you believe, by no means all are essential – but there are several articles, such as the ones shown on these two pages, that are virtually indispensable and will make it easier for you to work.

## Easels

Buying a good easel will make working on even a modest-sized support easier. It will also give you a psychological boost, inspiring you to greater things. There are several questions that you need to ask yourself when buying an easel. What size of work do you intend to produce? Are you going to use the easel on location or in the studio? If it is going to be used in your home or studio, is the room large enough?

The medium in which you like to work is also an important consideration. Oils are invariably painted with the support vertical, as are acrylics if used at the consistency of oil paint. However, if you are using fluid washes, then you will be working with the support horizontal, or nearly so, in order to prevent the paint from running. The same is invariably the case with gouache.

With any upright easel, stability is a primary consideration. Always test the stability of your chosen easel by placing on it the largest support that you intend to use.

Portable easels need to be lightweight, so that they can be easily transported, easy to erect and stable. They are usually made of wood, although a limited range is available in metal. Portable easels usually have three telescopically adjustable legs, so that you can set up the easel on uneven ground. The support is held between adjustable clamps and can be angled at any position from the horizontal to the vertical. Large portable easels can double as studio easels but they are generally not as stable.

A variation on this type of easel is the portable box easel, which incorporates a box that will hold all the equipment needed for a day's painting. Everything folds and packs away

**Table easels** ▲
The simplest table easels can be adjusted to hold a support horizontally or at varying angles up to about 45 degrees. They are perfect for working on gouache and acrylic paintings using thin, fluid paint.

**Portable box easel** ▶
Everything you need for a day's painting on location can be stored in the box beneath the easel.

neatly, while a carrying handle makes transportation easy. Some box easels even come with carrying straps, so that you can transport the easel on your back, like a rucksack – perfect for location work.

There is a comprehensive range of studio easels, with a model available to suit all styles and sizes of work. They are expensive, but a good studio easel will last a lifetime. Made of wood, studio easels are based around two distinct shapes – the A shape and the H shape. Both hold the support vertically.

H-shaped easels can handle larger canvases, with larger models being raised and lowered by means of a ratchet system. Some lighter-weight easels fold and convert into an easel that can hold a drawing board horizontally.

A-shaped easels are invariably smaller than H-shaped easels. They also fold flat easily, which makes them more suitable for use when space is at a premium. The height is adjusted by means of a series of catches that lock the support into position.

A less expensive alternative is the radial easel. These easels can hold a reasonably sized support. They have three short legs that give reasonable stability and can be adjusted in height.

◄ **Studio easel**
This is just one of many kinds of studio easel available. Buy one that is sturdy enough to hold a large canvas.

## Drawing boards

Unless you are working on a rigid board or stretched canvas, you will need a drawing board on to which you can secure or stretch your paper or watercolour board. Art stores stock boards made from thick, smooth plywood in a range of sizes. It is sometimes possible to find boards made from jointed timber with screwed cross-pieces in second-hand stores, and these are worth buying as they will last a lifetime.

There are also boards intended for location work, which have a long strap running diagonally across the board and can be placed over the shoulder and neck, allowing you to hold the board in position while you are standing, without using your hands.

## Mahl stick

Another useful piece of equipment when oil painting at an easel is a mahl stick, which consists of a light rod of wood (bamboo) with a soft leather ball secured on one end. This simple piece of equipment can be held in one hand and rested on the edge of the work. You can then rest your painting hand on the rod, which is positioned over the area being worked on. This steadies the hand, making it easier to do fine detailed work, and also keeps your painting hand clear of any wet paint so that you do not run the risk of smudging the paint.

If you do not want to go to the expense of buying a ready-made mahl stick, it is very easy to improvise and construct one yourself. Simply buy a length of dowelling or similar lightweight wood, wrap old rags around one end, and tape them in position with masking tape.

**Mahl stick ▼**
The mahl stick shown here comes in two parts, which can be screwed together to make one long stick so that it can be used when working on large canvases.

# Applying paint

Brushes are the obvious means of applying paint to the support, and a wide range is available. The marks they make depend on both the shape of the brush (round or flat) and the material from which it is made. Hogshair bristle, which is often used for oil and acrylics brushes, is stiff and relatively unbending, and creates definite-shaped marks, while the sable or synthetic/sable mixes used for gouache and watercolour brushes are more pliable and create a softer mark. Of course, you can also use watercolour and gouache brushes for acrylic paints if you are using the paint thinly.

There are also many other things that you can use to make marks. Some are designed specifically for painting, while others are everyday household items. Experiment to see what effects you can achieve. Dip fabrics, from coarse but evenly textured linen to pretty, delicate lace, into paint to transfer their patterns to the support; press twigs, pieces of cardboard, or even out-of-date credit cards into paint and scrape them over your painting surface to make straight lines; dip scrunched-up aluminium foil or plastic food wrap in paint and press it on to the support to make random textures; even apply paint with your fingers, just as you did when you were a child.

## Unusual paint applicators

There is a huge range of paint applicators on the market – some of which are useful, while others are little more than manufacturers' gimmicks. Each type makes a different kind of mark.

**Paint shaper** ▲
Available in a range of sizes and forms paint shapers consist of a shaped rubber tip fitted into a metal ferrule, which in turn is fitted into a wooden handle, just like a brush. The type of mark you can make depends on the size and shape of the tip. Paint shapers are best used with reasonably thick acrylic or oil paint; you can also use them with thin acrylic paint, gouache or watercolour.

**Foam roller** ▲
Foam paint rollers, like those used in household decoration, are a great way of covering a large area quickly – when you want to prepare a toned ground, for example. They can also be used to achieve textural effects. They are available in various sizes and are inexpensive enough to be discarded when they are too dirty to use.

**Foam brush** ▲
This consists of a wedge of synthetic foam attached to a handle. It can be dragged across the support to make broad marks in which the texture of the foam is evident. You can also dip the tip in the paint to make straight lines.

**Sponge** ▲
Sponges are a great way of creating texture for things like lichen on stone or random clouds and are particularly useful for landscape work. Synthetic sponges give a more even texture than the natural sponge shown here.

**Rag or paper** ▲
Rags and scrunched-up absorbent paper are used in the same way as sponges to create textured marks for particular subjects, although the textures that they create tend to be more irregular.

# Brushes for oils and acrylics

Brushes for oils and acrylics tend to be made from bristle, which is relatively hard and unyielding. This means that the marks tend to have a distinctive shape. Synthetic nylon brushes are much softer.

## Round brushes

**Short strokes** ▲
With the brush handle more or less parallel to the support, you can quickly build up an area of paint by making short strokes.

**Rounded marks** ▲
Holding the brush at 45 degrees to the support means that you are using the tip of the brush. This creates more rounded marks.

**Dots** ▲
Holding the brush almost perpendicular to the support and dabbing it on to the support creates small dots and stipples.

**Long strokes** ▲
Stroking the brush over the support as if you were drawing with a pencil allows you to make long, flowing marks.

**Rough, uneven texture** ▲
Scrubbing on paint using the side of the brush creates a rough, uneven texture that is ideal when you want to cover a large area but do not want a flat wash of colour.

## Flat brushes

**Long strokes** ▲
Making long strokes with a flat brush held parallel to the support, the wedge-like shape of the brush head is evident.

**Short strokes** ▲
Short, wedge-shaped strokes can be used to deliver thick paint to the support – a technique used to create heavy impasto.

**Dots** ▲
Holding the brush almost perpendicular to the support and dabbing it on to the support creates short lines and wedge-shaped marks.

**Thin strokes** ▲
Use the edge of the brush to make thin marks, applying light pressure so as not to splay the bristles. The marks can be straight or curved.

**Rough, uneven texture** ▲
Scrubbing on paint using the side of the brush creates a rough, uneven texture in the same way as with a round brush and is useful for scumbling one colour over another.

# Brushes for gouache

The brushes used for gouache tend to be the same as those used for pure watercolour – soft sable and sable/synthetic mixes. For control and fine mark making, make sure that you buy brushes that hold their shape well. Although sable brushes are more expensive than synthetics, they will last longer if you look after them.

## Round brushes

**Short strokes** ▲
Made using the point of the brush and, depending on the amount of pressure applied, short strokes are reasonably even in width.

**Rounded marks** ▲
Dabbing the end of the brush on to the support produces blob-like dots, the size of which depend on the consistency of the paint.

## Flat brushes

**Long strokes** ▲
Dragging the whole width of the brush over the support while applying even pressure results in a mark of an even width.

**Short strokes** ▲
Made using only the top half of the brush, short strokes create even and relatively broad rectangular-shaped marks.

**Applying pressure** ▲
Holding the brush almost perpendicular to the support and applying pressure splays out the bristles, creating broad marks.

**Long strokes** ▲
As with oil and acrylic brushes, stroking the brush over the support and applying steady pressure makes flowing marks of even width.

**Fine marks** ▲
Holding the brush upright and dabbing it lightly on to the support results in a thin, often slightly curved mark the width of the brush tip.

**Long strokes using one edge of the brush** ▲
For fine lines, use only one edge of the brush rather than the whole width and apply steady pressure.

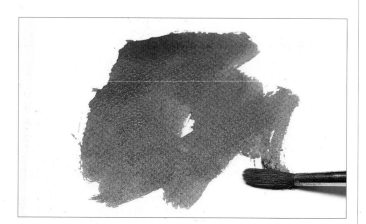

**Rough, uneven texture** ▲
Scrubbing on paint using the side of the brush creates a rough, uneven texture that allows some of the support or underlying paint layer to be seen.

**Uneven texture** ▲
As with the other brushes, scrubbing on paint using the side of the brush rather than the tip creates a random, uneven texture in which individual brushmarks cannot be discerned.

# Painting knives

Painting knives are available in several shapes and sizes, in both metal and plastic. They are ideal for thick, impasto-like applications. Painting knives are generally used for oils and acrylics, although it is also possible to use gouache straight from the tube; however, the texture will not be as pronounced as when using oils or acrylics.

## Painting knives using oils and acrylics

**Broad marks ▲**
Spreading paint on to the canvas with the flat of the knife, as one would when icing a cake, creates a flat, even application of paint.

**Press on and lift off ▲**
Pressing the knife on to the support and then lifting it off, without dragging it, makes marks that echo the shape of the knife.

**Dots ▲**
Dotting the tip of the knife on to the support creates short, sharp marks that are useful for detail and adding highlights.

**Uneven lines ▲**
Because the paint is thick and does not spread evenly, dragging the tip of the knife across the support creates lines that vary in width.

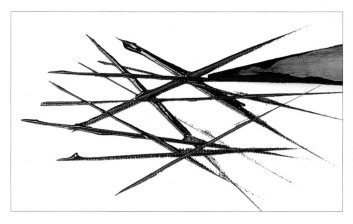

**Thin strokes using the knife edge ▲**
Turning the knife on its edge and pressing it on to the support, or dragging it across the surface, creates thinner lines that are even in width – a good technique for straight edges.

## Painting knives for gouache

**Broad marks ▲**
For broad marks, smear the paint over the paper using the flat of the knife. The technique is exactly the same as for oils and acrylics.

**Short marks ▲**
Pressing one flat edge of the knife on to the paper and smearing the mark a little creates short marks the width of the knife.

**Dots ▲**
Dotting the tip of the knife on to the paper creates fine points that could be used to depict pollen inside a flower, leaves on trees, or highlights.

**Long, uneven marks ▲**
Using the edge of the knife and angling it at about 45 degrees to the paper creates long, uneven marks that are good for loose, linear work.

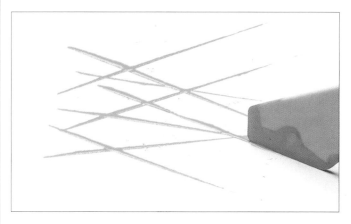

**Press on and lift off ▲**
Pressing one sharp edge of the knife at an angle of 90 degrees creates a crisp, clean line of even width on the paper. To make longer lines pull the knife across the support.

# Tone

If you want to show that an object is three-dimensional, you need to master the art of depicting tone. Tone is simply the relative lightness or darkness of a colour. Another term that you may come across in art books is "value" – but the meaning is exactly the same.

The apparent lightness or darkness of a subject depends on several things. First, it depends on the quality, intensity and direction of the light source: if one side of an object is brightly lit (for example, a still life illuminated by sunlight streaming in through a window to the side of the set-up), it will be lighter in value than the side that is in shadow or shielded from the light. Second, the tone depends on the relative lightness or darkness of the colours present within that subject.

In order to create the illusion of three-dimensional form on a flat, two-dimensional surface, more than one tone needs to be in evidence. If you draw a circle and paint it a uniform mid-tone red, all you will see is a flat red disc. If, however, you paint one side of your circle red and then gradually darken that red colour as

you paint across the circle to the other side, the circle appears to become a sphere, one side apparently hit by the light and the other side in shadow.

In general, strong light makes colours appear brighter and more intense. It also increases the tonal gap, or the range of tones evident between the lightest tone and the darkest. This is known as contrast. An image with a strong tonal contrast will look more three-dimensional and appear to have greater depth than an image that lacks contrast. Used well, tone can also play an important part in conveying mood and atmosphere.

Colour also has an important part to play when you are assessing tonal values. When you are painting an image, a black object in bright light still needs to look black, just as a white object in shadow still needs to look white. A light-coloured object in bright light or deep shadow will look lighter than a dark colour in light or shade. In reality, however, very different colours can have the same tonal value, with even comparatively light colours looking surprisingly dark in the right lighting

conditions. Perhaps the best way to appreciate this is to look at a black-and-white photograph, where colours that are very different can look tonally the same or very similar.

Pure hues have distinct tonal values. Prussian blue is very dark in value, while lemon yellow is very light. This is best seen when positioning a hue against its matching tonal value on a value scale. However, similar hues can have very different tonal values, while different hues can be very similar in tone.

A pure hue straight from the tube is usually made darker by adding black or a mixture of other colours. A colour is lightened by adding white.

**Colours and tonal equivalents** ▼
Although there are hundreds of tonal values between black and white, the brain can only distinguish the differences between a few – as shown in the tonal scale, below. The second row shows the tonal equivalent – the relative lightness or darkness – of a number of different hues.

◀ **Darkening colours**
To darken a colour, add black.

◀ **Lightening colours**
To lighten a colour, add white.

## Practice exercise: **Seeing in tones**

This exercise, painted in shades of grey, provides the opportunity to translate colours into tone. You may be surprised to discover that colours that you think of as being very different – the red of the pepper and chillies and the green of the broccoli, for example, or the red and dark blue of the cloth – are very similar in tone. Note, too, how many variations in tone there are within one colour – for example, in the white areas of the cloths and on the white plate. These differences are essential in conveying a feeling of light and shade.

In this exercise, the very brightest areas are left unpainted. Start by working out where these are, and then where the next lightest tone occurs. Working from light to dark in this way allows you to build up the tones very gradually. Remember that acrylic paint looks slightly darker when it is dry than it does when it is wet. Test all your mixtures first by applying them to a piece of scrap paper or board and waiting for them to dry.

It's often hard to be sure in the early stages that you've got things right, so be prepared to re-assess matters once you've put down several tones then make adjustments if necessary.

### Materials
- *B pencil*
- *Canvas board*
- *Acrylic paints: Mars black, titanium white*
- *Brushes: small flat*

### The set-up
This still life contains all three primary colours – red, yellow and blue – as well as black and white. The tablecloths and the lemons may turn out to be much darker than you might imagine, while even the darkest object (the aubergine [eggplant]) contains areas of bright highlight that help to define its form.

1 Using a B pencil, lightly sketch the subject. Put in as much detail as you need: although it's quite time-consuming to draw the checks of the cloths, for example, they will enable you to place the shifts in tone accurately. Similarly, the highlights on the vegetables will help you to define their form.

2 Mix the lightest tone from Mars black and titanium white. Using a small flat brush, paint the highlights on the aubergine, broccoli stalk, peppers and cloths. Use the same tone for the garlic, lemons and the blade of the topmost knife, except for the very brightest highlights.

▶

**3** Look carefully to see where apparently uniform colours change tone. Add a little black to the mixture to darken it slightly and paint the cast shadows on the plate, the shaded edges of the lemons and the broccoli florets. Go over the first tone where necessary to darken it.

**4** Now add more black to the paint mixture for your third tone. Darken the individual segments and the papery top of the garlic. Brush tone 3 over the wooden table and chopping board and around the main subject, taking care to cut around any light areas.

**5** The chopping board is darker than the table on which it rests, so add still more black to the paint to make tone 4 and go over the chopping board again. Use the same tone to deepen the shadows on the peppers and chillies. Also use it to paint the rivets on the knife handles and the blade of the lower knife, which is somewhat tarnished and darker in tone.

 **Tip**: When assessing tones, half-close your eyes: you will be able to see the differences more clearly.

**6** If you think the highlights that you put down in the early stages look too pale – as here on the yellow pepper, for example – darken them a little. Add more black to make tone 5. Using short brushstrokes, dab the paint over the broccoli florets, leaving some of the underlying tone showing through in places. Use the same tone on the large red pepper and chillies, leaving the highlights untouched, and on the blue-and-white cloth in the background.

**7** Still using tone 5, continue working on the cloths. Note how the direction of the stripes changes with the folds in the cloth. Paint a thin shadow under the edge of the chopping board; this helps to separate it from the table and defines its form. Painting around the rivets, paint the dark wooden handle of the topmost knife.

**Tip**: You may find it helps to switch to a smaller brush, as you're working on very small, crisply defined areas at this stage in the painting.

**8** Add more black to make tone 6 and paint the darkest parts of the blue-and-white cloth – the squares where two blue bands overlap. Paint the aubergine, brushing around the light areas, and the handle of the lower knife.

**9** Using tone 6, darken the left-hand side of the red pepper. Add more black to make the darkest tone. Paint a thin strip along the top of the topmost knife. Use the same tone for the darkest parts of the aubergine and chilli peppers.

### The finished painting

In this painting, seven tones plus the white of the support have been used to create a convincingly three-dimensional portrayal of a multi-coloured still life. It is interesting that colours that appear to be very different from one another (the red of the peppers and the green of the broccoli florets, for example) turn out to be very similar in tone. When you've done this exercise, you might like to try setting up another multi-coloured still life. Although it might seem difficult at first, you will quickly become adept at interpreting colours as tones; it is a vital part of making your paintings look rounded and three-dimensional.

The pale green of the broccoli stalk is almost the same tone as the yellow pepper, although you might expect it to be considerably darker.

The darkest part of the chilli is almost as dark as the aubergine, although you might expect it to be lighter in tone.

Don't assume that things you know to be white will actually appear pure white: as you can see, some tone is evident in the white of the cloth.

# Scaling up

People often paint from photographs. Some artists argue that this kills spontaneity, as there's a risk that you end up slavishly copying rather than interpreting what's in front of your eyes, but it's a perfectly valid way of painting. It isn't always practical to paint a scene from life, and photographs give you the opportunity to collect reference material when you're on your travels, or simply going about your daily business, and then work them up into a painting at your own convenience.

Some artists also make a small-scale sketch before they start on the painting itself. There are several reasons for doing this. First, it is a good way of deciding on the best composition: a quick sketch establishes the work's centre of interest and shows how the different elements of the scene relate to one another. Second, it enables you to work out the tonal values of the scene. This is just as important in colour work as it is in a monochrome drawing or pen-and-ink work, as an accurate assessment of tones is one of the things that will make your painting look three-dimensional.

But whether you're painting from a photo or from life, once you've got your reference material how do you transfer it on to a larger canvas or support?

It takes a certain amount of confidence to do this purely by eye, without any guidelines to help you – although, like anything else, you'll get better with practice. Luckily, there is a tried-and-tested means of scaling up. It involves superimposing a grid on your preliminary sketch or photo and marking a larger grid on your canvas. You can then copy the scene, one square at a time, and the lines of the grid will give you a good guide to where to position things. You can see, for example, that your subject's eye or the edge of a vase coincides with the edge of the second square down – so all you have to do is make sure that you draw it in the same position in your larger grid.

In a complicated scene such as a building or an elaborate still life, you might want to subdivide some of the squares. Any method that enables you to keep track of where you are in the sketch is fine.

**Acetate grid over photograph** ▲
Draw a grid on acetate (available from craft and art supply stores) and place it over your photograph. Then draw a grid on your paper or canvas, keeping the same proportions. If, for example, the grid on your photo is five squares across and four squares down, the grid on your canvas should be the same – although the squares will be larger. You can then transfer the contents of each square in turn to make your underdrawing or sketch.

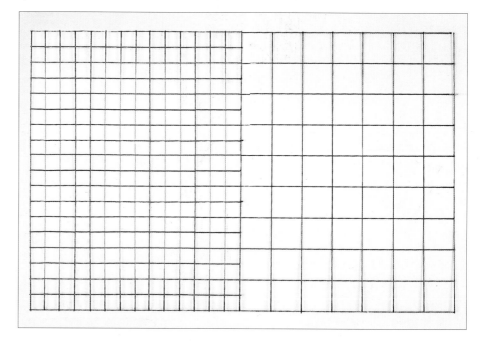

**Different-sized squares within the same grid** ▲
In areas where you need more guidelines, simply divide the squares of the grid into smaller squares.

## Practice exercise: **Scaling up a small sketch**

The method for scaling up a small composition sketch is exactly the same as for scaling up a photograph. If, for example, the grid on your sketch is five squares across and four squares down, the grid on your canvas should contain the same number of squares – although they will be larger than the squares on the sketch. The grid system can also be used to make a drawing or sketch smaller, simply by reducing the size at which the grid is drawn on the support.

**1** First make your initial sketch freehand and divide it up with a grid of evenly sized squares. The number of squares is up to you, but they should all be the same size.

**2** Then lightly mark a grid on the canvas on which you're going to make your painting, keeping the same proportions. Lightly mark the main intersections – the points where the edges of your subject touch on the lines of the grid.

**3** Start joining up the intersections, working square by square and referring continually to your initial sketch to check that each shape is occupying the same area on your canvas as it did on the sketch. Already, your subject is beginning to take shape.

**4** Continue transferring information until your underdrawing is complete. At this point, if you wish, you can also put in some shading to act as a tonal guide.

**The finished underdrawing**
When you have put down as much information as you need, you can begin the process of painting. The amount of detail that you put into your underdrawing depends at least in part on the complexity of your subject and is entirely up to you. Remember that an underdrawing is merely a guide to help you place elements correctly and work out the tones.

# Underdrawing

An underdrawing is exactly what it says – a preliminary sketch on the canvas or paper, over which you paint your picture. Although some artists launch straight into a painting, most people – particularly if they are new to painting – like the reassurance that an underdrawing provides. It allows you to set down the lines of your subject, and erase and change them if necessary, before you commit yourself irrevocably to paint.

Your approach to the underdrawing will depend partly on the medium in which you're working. If you're painting in a transparent or relatively transparent medium such as watercolour or thin acrylic paint, you need to make sure that your underdrawing is light enough to be covered by the subsequent layers of paint. With thicker and opaque mediums, such as oils or impasto acrylics, the underdrawing can be heavier.

The style of your underdrawing also depends on the subject. If you're painting buildings, for example, it's important to get the angles of the roofs and windows right – so you might want to make a fairly detailed underdrawing that gives you plenty of guidelines to follow when you start to apply the paint. The same might apply to a complicated still life, in which lots of different elements overlap each other. For a loose, impressionistic landscape, on the other hand, a few sweeping lines might suffice.

But providing linear guidelines to follow is only one function of an underdrawing. It should also give you information about the tonal range of the scene, so that you know where the light and dark areas are. This can be in the form of loose scribbles and cross-hatching that roughly define the different areas.

For most purposes, an ordinary pencil is all you need, but it is not your only option. The underdrawings on these two pages are all made in different mediums, chosen for a specific reason.

### Underdrawing in charcoal ▼

The lovely sweeping lines of the ground and foliage, counterbalanced by the strong upright lines of the tree trunks, are what attracted the artist to this subject. The intention is to produce an atmospheric landscape, in which an overall impression of the scene is more important than precisely rendered detail. Charcoal is perfect for this, as you can make broad sweeping strokes across the support using the side of the charcoal. It is also superb for blocking in areas of dark tone. To prevent the charcoal from mixing with the paint and muddying the colours, always brush off any excess, and spray fixative (available from all art supply stores) over the underdrawing.

## Underdrawing in pencil ▲

Architectural subjects generally require quite a detailed underdrawing: whenever you are painting buildings in two-point perspective, as here, it's vital that you get all the angles right and position all the different elements (windows, chimneys and so on) correctly in relation to one another. A complicated still life is another subject where the relations between one object and its neighbours are critical. A sharp pencil allows you to do this and cross-hatch small, more densely shaded areas such as the window recesses and foliage. It also produces a relatively light underdrawing that will easily be covered by subsequent layers of paint.

## Underdrawing in acrylic paint ▶

The boundary between an underdrawing and an underpainting is sometimes blurred, but if we define an underdrawing as a linear approach, then this certainly qualifies. The brush has been used in the same way as a pencil or pen to indicate the tilt of the head and body and the position of the facial features. There is also some indication of tone within the subject. The choice of burnt sienna is an appropriate one, as it hints at the warm flesh tones of the subject.

# Underpainting

The main difference between an under-drawing and an underpainting is that the former is primarily linear in approach while the latter provides more tonal information by roughly blocking in the main shapes and tones before applying colour. Whether you choose to make an underdrawing or an underpainting is entirely a matter of personal choice. Both, however, enable you to work out your composition and the tonal structure of the scene before you begin to apply colour and refine the detail of your subject.

Underpaintings are used in both oil and acrylic paintings. In both mediums, the colour is diluted to a thin consistency – oils with turpentine or other thinner, acrylics with water to which matt medium has been added – to prevent any shine on the underpainting. Because the paint is so thin, alterations can be made by wiping a turpentine- or water-soaked rag, depending on the medium, over the paint – something that is much more difficult to do in the later stages of a painting, when the paint has been applied more thickly.

Underpaintings for works in acrylic must always be made in acrylic paint. Under-paintings for works in oils can be made either in acrylics (provided the support has previously been primed with an acrylic primer) or oils. The benefit of using acrylics for the underpainting, of course, is that they are fast drying. Even fast-drying oil colours, such as flake white and diluted earth colours, need to be left to dry for a couple of days, while a thin acrylic underpainting will dry in a matter of minutes.

## Colours for underpaintings

Many artists favour the traditional method of making a monochrome underpainting in neutral colours, generally greys or browns.

Others block in the light and dark tones in a rough approximation of the final colours. This allows you to check the overall colour balance of the work at a very early stage.

A third approach is to use a contrasting or complementary colour for the underpainting. The great Flemish artist Peter Paul Rubens (1577–1640), for example, often used terre verte (a muted green) as the underpainting colour in his nudes, as it complements the pink flesh tones and cools the shadows.

## Practice exercise: **Monochrome underpainting**

The advantage of a monochrome underpainting is that it enables you to concentrate on tone rather than colour. It also provides a tonal base for any subsequent glazing technique. Work boldly without putting in textural detail.

### Materials
- Acrylic paper
- Acrylic paints: ivory black, titanium white
- Brushes: small flat

### The set-up
The tones in this still life need to be carefully assessed if the objects are to be made to look convincingly three-dimensional. Set up a table lamp to one side of the still life, so that the objects cast strong and clearly defined shadows, as this will make it easier for you to assess both the direction and the intensity of the light – and hence to work out the relative tones of the various objects.

1 Mix a light grey and loosely draw in the outline of the lemons and the pot. Darken the tone slightly and block in the pot.

2 Apply the same tone to the inside of the pot, which is in shadow, and to the shaded sides of the lemons, again roughly blocking in the colour.

**3** Add a little more black to the mixture to darken it further, and indicate the shadows cast by the lemons. Use the same mixture to paint in the outer rim of the shaded side of the pot.

**4** Darken the inside lip of the pot and paint in the darker reflections and the shadows cast on its outer surface. Use the same mixture to apply a tone over the area of shadow on the left of the image.

**5** Add white to the mixture to make a very light grey and paint the lightest area of the image – the brightly lit backdrop on the right of the still life. Complete the blocking in by using white on the highlights.

## The completed underpainting

The underpainting has deliberately been kept loose and sketchy in style, but it has allowed the artist to work out his composition and it provides all the tonal information needed to make a more detailed and resolved painting. Once you have worked out the tonal structure of the still life, you can think about putting in the colour and textural detail.

The darkest areas are only roughly blocked in: this is simply a preliminary to making the painting, so do not attempt to smooth out brushstrokes or put in any kind of detailing.

The very brightest areas can be painted as pure white.

# Toned grounds

Some artists like to paint on a coloured, or toned, ground rather than on white canvas or paper. There are two main reasons for doing this. First, it can be difficult to judge colours against a white ground, particularly in the early stages of a painting when there are few, if any, other colours on the support to which you can relate them. In this situation, most colours tend to look darker than they really are – and so you may overcompensate by making your mixes lighter than they should be. If you start on a mid-toned, neutral-coloured ground, however, it is much easier to assess tones correctly.

Second, working on a toned ground establishes an overall colour "key" or mood for your painting. If you allow the colour of the ground to show through in places, it helps to unify the painting.

A toned ground may be either transparent or opaque. On a transparent ground, some of the colour of the support is reflected back up through the paint, giving a more luminous, vibrant feel to the painting. For this method, the paint should be heavily diluted (with water for acrylic or gouache paints, or with a thinner such as turpentine or household white spirit for oil paints), and spread over the support in a thin layer, using a brush or a lint-free rag. An opaque ground is used with opaque painting methods such as impasto, where the influence of the white ground is not so important. For an opaque ground, mix your chosen colour with either white paint or primer.

Acrylic paints dry quickly, whereas an oil ground may take a whole day or even longer to dry. To speed things up, many oil painters tone the ground with acrylic paint. (It is possible to paint oils on top of acrylics, but not the opposite way around, as this is likely to make the paint crack.)

What colour should you use to tone the ground? Some artists use a colour that is in keeping with the subject – a warm pink or orange for a nude study, or earth colours for a landscape. Others prefer a contrast, such as a hint of yellow beneath a brilliant blue sky or a reddish brown to warm up a landscape. Opt for a neutral tone that is mid-way between the lightest and darkest values in your painting.

## How to tone a ground

Whether you apply paint with a rag or with a brush is largely a matter of personal preference. The important thing is to use a thin layer of paint. It doesn't matter if some brushes' strokes are visible or if the paint is slightly streaked; in fact, this gives a more lively, spontaneous effect.

### Applying paint with a rag

1 Dab your chosen colour (which can be oil or acrylic) over the canvas.

2 Dip a rag in the appropriate thinner (white spirit, turpentine or low-odour thinner for oil paint; water for acrylics), and rub the rag over the canvas to spread the paint over the surface. It is a good idea to wear rubber gloves. Leave to dry.

**The prepared ground** ▲

### Applying paint with a brush

1 This method can be used with oils, acrylics or gouache. Mix a thin wash of your chosen colour and, using a large, flat brush, apply the paint to the surface, varying the direction of the brushstrokes.

**The prepared ground** ▲
Always allow the prepared, toned ground to dry completely before you begin your painting.

> **Tip**: When choosing a colour for your toned ground, whether you decide to go for a neutral grey or a toning or a contrasting colour, opt for a neutral tone that is midway between the lightest and darkest values in your painting. Soft colours – earth colours such as raw sienna or burnt umber, or soft blues, blue-greys and greens – tend to work well.

## Practice exercise: **Teapot on a warm ground**

For your first attempts at using a toned ground, try painting a simple subject on different colours of ground to see what difference it makes. You will probably find that the differences are quite subtle; nonetheless, the colour of the ground will have an impact on the overall mood and colour temperature of the painting.

In this exercise, the artist decided to work on a warm ground that would complement the colour of the copper lustre teapot. The warm underpainting also serves to accentuate the coolness of the blues used to paint the background and table cloth. She then went on to paint the same subject on a white and a blue ground; the results can be seen overleaf.

**Materials**
- *Acrylic paper*
- *HB pencil*
- *Acrylic paints: burnt sienna, cerulean blue, titanium white, phthalocyanine green, ultramarine blue, cadmium red, cadmium yellow, alizarin crimson*
- *Brushes: medium flat, small round, fine round or rigger*

**The set-up**
Choose a simple subject on a plain background – but look for an interesting interplay of colours and tones.

1 First, tone the support with burnt sienna acrylic paint. It doesn't matter if the coverage is slightly uneven. Leave to dry, then sketch your subject using an HB pencil.

2 Mix a very pale blue from cerulean blue and titanium white. Using a medium flat brush, block in the background above the table. The pale blue serves as a complementary colour to the burnt sienna ground and the contrast between the two gives the painting more impact.

3 Mix a bluish green from phthalocyanine green, ultramarine blue and titanium white and paint the cloth on which the pot is resting, darkening the mixture by adding more green for the shadow cast by the teapot's spout. Use the same colour for the inner edge of the handle and a very dilute version of the mixture for the cooler areas within the teapot, where the colour of the cloth is reflected up into the metallic glaze.

▶

4 Mix a pale, yellowish gold from cadmium red, cadmium yellow and titanium white. Using a small round brush, put in the very brightest, irregularly shaped highlights, where light is hitting the glazed surface of the teapot. Note that the colour of the highlights is applied as a very thin layer of paint; consequently, it is slightly modified by the underlying burnt sienna of the ground.

5 Mix a dark purple from alizarin crimson and ultramarine blue. Using a fine round or rigger brush, "draw" a very fine line around the lid to imply the shaded recess in which the lid sits. Use the same colour to paint the thin line of shadow under the pot. Add more phthalocyanine green to the bluish green mixture from Step 3 and paint the reflections of the cloth at the base of the pot.

### The finished painting
The burnt sienna ground gives an overall warmth and richness to the painting, as can be seen in the background, where hints of it remain visible through the thin blue-white paint.

It also serves as the deepest copper colour within the pot; the ground colour has not been painted over in these sections and this helps to unify the painting.

Hints of the toned ground remain visible through the thin blue-white mixture used to paint the background.

The burnt sienna ground is not completely covered over; here, it serves as the deepest copper colour within the pot.

### White ground ▶

The artist also painted the same scene on a white ground. A white ground tends to reflect a certain amount of light, even through a relatively opaque colour, which has the effect of making the overall key lighter. There is less interplay of colours within the metallic glaze of the pot and the highlights have been left as white, rather than painted on later.

### Blue ground ▼

The version painted on a blue ground is cooler in mood. However, the blue ground is a good complementary colour for the coppery pot. Even small areas of blue underpainting, if allowed to show through, will have an effect on any adjacent colours.

# Washes

Laying a wash – a thin layer of transparent colour – is common practice in both gouache and acrylic painting, just as it is in watercolour painting. (The nearest equivalent in oil painting is glazing.) The idea is to apply fluid, thinned paint over areas that are too large to be covered by a single brushstroke. Washes are often used to form a base colour over which the image is then developed. As this tends to involve working over a large area, or even covering the whole of the support, always mix far more paint than you think you'll need: it's surprising how quickly you use it up, and if you run out, it can be very difficult to re-mix exactly the same shade. Before you apply the paint, prop your drawing board up on the easel at a slight angle, so that the paint can flow easily down the paper.

When using gouache paint or acrylic thinned with water and applied in the same way as watercolour, there are various types of wash. A flat wash is a smooth, even layer of colour with no discernible differences in tone or visible brushmarks. In a gradated wash, the colour shades from dark to light (or vice versa). A variegated wash, as the name suggests, consists of more than one colour. All washes are applied in a similar way, with the paint either merging wet into wet into another colour or spreading naturally over a damp support.

The main difference between gouache (or watercolour) and acrylic washes stems from the way in which the paints are manufactured. In gouache and watercolour paints the pigments are bound with gum, which holds them together even when they are diluted with water to the point where the paint appears to be virtually colourless. In acrylic paints the pigments are bound with an acrylic resin, which gives the paint body and substance; but if the paint is diluted too much, it begins to break down and any wash will look thin and lifeless. Because the paint has body, acrylic washes are easier to control than watercolour and gouache. When using acrylic paint as a thin wash on canvas or board, add either a flow-improving medium or a retarding medium so that the thin paint brushes out evenly.

## Laying a wash

This sequence demonstrates the technique of laying a flat wash and is the same for acrylics, gouache and watercolour. When you are working in acrylics, however, it is a good idea to add a little flow-improving medium, as this increases the flow of the paint; very thin paint tends to puddle rather than brush out evenly across a surface. For a gradated wash, add more water to the paint as you work down the paper. For a variegated wash, change to a different colour part way through.

1 Using a large wash brush and working from left to right, lay a smooth stroke of colour across the paper. Quickly re-load your brush with more paint. Pick up the pool of paint at the base of the first stroke with your brush and continue across the paper, again working from left to right.

2 Continue until you have covered the paper. The paint should dry to a flat, even tone with no variation or visible brushmarks.

## Practice exercise: **Italian landscape**

In any landscape, open spaces are essential: the viewer's eye needs somewhere to rest after taking in the detail of trees, hills and other features. In this exercise, such spaces are provided by the series of flat washes laid over the paper, which also help to lead our eye through the scene.

Note how the tone deepens and becomes warmer with each successive wash: this is a classic device in landscape painting and a very simple way of creating a feeling of recession, as colours generally look paler and slightly cooler the further away things are.

### Materials
- *Watercolour board*
- *B pencil*
- *Acrylic paints: cadmium red, cerulean blue, ultramarine blue, olive green, cadmium yellow*
- *Flow-improving medium*
- *Brushes: large round, medium round, small round*

### The scene
Here we are looking into the sun and so the scene appears somewhat hazy. This makes it easier to paint: relatively little detail is discernible, so you can get away with painting generalized shapes and concentrate on assessing the tones correctly.

1 Using a B pencil, sketch the scene so that you have some guides for placing the main features. You don't need to include a lot of detail, but put in the outlines of the hills and the main trees and clumps of vegetation.

**Tip**: Successively darker washes will create a sense of recession in the landscape, so you don't need to include a lot of tonal information in the drawing.

2 Using a large round brush, wash very pale, dilute cadmium red over the sky. The colour is so pale that is it barely perceptible, but it adds warmth to the image. Wash very pale cerulean blue mixed with a few drops of flow-improving medium loosely over the sky. Add more paint to the mixture to darken it and paint the most distant range of hills. Darken it still further by adding ultramarine blue and a tiny amount of cadmium red and brush in the next line of hills. Mix a dark green from cerulean blue and olive green and paint the next range. With just four simple washes, the landscape is already beginning to take on a sense of depth.

**3** Wash olive green over the foreground, darkening the colour by adding cadmium red as you move down the paper. The warmer colour brings this area of the painting forwards and suggests the earth showing through the vegetation.

**4** While the foreground is still slightly damp, mix dark and mid-toned greens from varying proportions of olive green and cerulean blue, and using a small round brush, put in the main areas of vegetation. Use vertical brushstrokes for the cypress trees along the horizon and dab the paint on using a circular motion of the brush for the main wooded area on the left.

**5** Mix a mid-green from olive green and ultramarine blue and, using a small brush, block in the shapes of the cypress trees in the middle distance, just below the nearest range of hills. Because the underlying paper has dried out quite considerably by this stage, the paint you add now does not spread over the surface and the trees retain their neat, crisp shapes.

**7** Mix a warm brown from olive green and cadmium red and, using a medium round brush, dot this mixture into the foliage areas. Use the same mixture to paint furrows and shadows on the land.

**6** Continue putting in the mid-green detail in the middle distance, using the same colours as before and alternating between the different greens on your palette as appropriate. Paint the shadows cast by the trees in a neutral grey created by mixing cadmium red and ultramarine blue. With just a few washes and simple strokes, the scene is already turning into a delightful little landscape.

**Tip**: The trees are so far away that little detail is evident. A general impression of their shapes and tones, created by applying small blobs of paint and using short brushstrokes, is sufficient. When painting any type of vegetation, your brushstrokes should follow the direction in which the plant grows – so short vertical strokes are perfect for the cypress trees.

**8** Mix a very dark green from ultramarine blue and olive green and dab it into the wooded area on the left. Again, generalized shapes are sufficient.

**9** Wash the brown mixture from Step 7 over the foreground, adding some cadmium yellow to the mixture when you come to paint the immediate foreground. The warmth of the yellow has the effect of bringing this area forwards in the painting and makes it seem closer to the viewer.

**10** Mix a dark brownish green from olive green and cadmium red. Using a small round brush and loose strokes, put in the trees in the foreground. You can use thicker, more textured, paint here: along with the darker colour, this is another means of making the area appear closer to the viewer.

### The finished painting

Washes form the basis of this charming and atmospheric Italian landscape, and the detail of the trees and other vegetation is developed over the top once the washes are dry.

The tones of the washes have been carefully chosen to create a feeling of recession, while the earth colours in the foreground give a sense of warmth.

Areas of flat colour provide a resting space for the eye of the viewer.

Note how the washes become darker and warmer in tone as we move towards the foreground.

# Wet into wet and blending

Allowing one wet paint colour to merge into another on the support is a very exciting way of painting and it can create some extremely atmospheric effects. The thinner the paint, be it oil, acrylic or gouache, the more the different colours will bleed into one another.

With gouache and acrylic paints mixed with lots of water, the technique is akin to that used in watercolour painting and the result depends on how wet the first colour is. If the first colour is still very wet, any subsequent colour will spread and blur, and the result will be soft and somewhat hazy – perfect for subjects such as skies or reflections in water. If the first colour or the support has dried a little, however, the paint will not spread so far – and the brush marks will have a harder edge.

Working wet into wet in this way will always be slightly unpredictable – but that is one of the charms of the technique and, with practice, you will get better at judging how far the paint is likely to spread.

Oil paints, even when mixed with relatively large amounts of thinner, tend to have a certain amount of body and they do not spread on the support in the same way. However, because oil paints take such a long time to dry, you can blend wet colours together on the canvas with the brush to create both optical and physical colour mixes.

In landscapes, this is a useful technique for certain atmospheric effects, such as clouds and fog. It is also invaluable when you are painting subjects with subtle transitions from one tone to another – skin tones, for example, or soft fabrics in a still life. The amount of blending that you do is up to you. It is possible to blend colours so smoothly that the brushstrokes and the transition from one tone to another are virtually imperceptible; alternatively, you can loosely brush one wet colour over another, so that the two retain their own identity but appear to be mixed when the painting is viewed from a distance. Such optical mixes often create a more lively effect than physical mixes.

Very thin oil paints mixed with thinner but no added oil are often used to block in a painting. As the thinner evaporates, the paint dries sufficiently to allow further work, using progressively thicker paint, after a relatively short period of time.

## On a wet base colour ▼

If the first colour is still very wet, any subsequent colour will spread, blurring at the edges. The extent of the spread depends on how wet the underlying colour is; this is something that you will learn to judge with practice.

## Blending paint with a fan brush

Thick oil and acrylic paints can be blended on the support, rather than in the palette, to create another colour. This technique is very effective where subtle gradations of colour are required.

**1** Put the two colours down separately on the support. Here, we used cadmium red and cadmium yellow.

**2** Using a fan brush, gently stroke one colour into the other so that the two blend together.

**3** The two colours merge physically on the support to create a third colour – here, orange.

## Blending wet acrylic paint with water

When acrylic paint touches an area that is already wet, it will spread and blur within the wet area. If you do not want this to happen, make sure you allow colours to dry throughly before applying an adjacent one!

1 Put the first colour down on the support and leave it to dry. Brush clean water over part of the first colour.

2 Apply the second colour, painting up to the edge of the area that you wetted with clean water.

3 The second colour spreads into the wet area and mixes optically to create orange.

## Practice exercise: **Autumn leaves**

In this exercise, red and green paints are allowed to merge into each other, blending together on the support to create subtle, soft-edged shifts from one colour to the next. Painting autumn leaves is a great way of practising the wet-into-wet technique, as you don't need to be terribly precise about where one colour ends and the next one begins.

### Materials
- *Watercolour board*
- *2B pencil*
- *Acrylic paints: alizarin crimson, cadmium yellow, phthalocyanine green, titanium white*
- *Brushes: large round, fine round*

### The scene
These vine leaves are just beginning to turn from a glossy green to a rich red.

1 Using a 2B pencil, lightly sketch the outline of the leaves and the main veins.

> **Tip**: This is a relatively simple scene in which the tones on the leaves will be built up wet into wet, so all you need to do at this stage is delineate the shapes within which you'll be working.

2 Mix a warm, dilute red from alizarin crimson and a little cadmium yellow. Using a large, round brush, loosely brush the mixture over the red parts of the leaves. You don't need to be very precise about where you place the red, but try not to allow paint to spill outside the leaves.

▶

3 Mix a bright green from cadmium yellow and phthalocyanine green. While the red paint is wet, brush the mixture over the brightest green leaves, allowing it to merge into the red. Add more phthalocyanine green to darken the mixture, and paint the leaves on the bottom right of the image.

4 Mix a very dark green from phthalocyanine green and alizarin crimson. Using a fine round brush, put in the most prominent veins. Hold the brush by the end of the handle, almost vertically to the support, and lightly touch it on to the support to get some variation in the line.

5 Mix a dark red from alizarin crimson and a little phthalocyanine green and outline the edges of some of the redder leaves.

6 Using the dark green from Step 4, block in the spaces between the leaves. While the paint is still wet, mix some alizarin crimson into the dark green and drop it into the spaces, wet into wet. This looks much more interesting than a flat wash of a single colour as dark shadow areas are rarely, if ever, uniform in colour.

7 Continue working on the dark, shadowy spaces between the leaves. Defining these spaces will make the shapes of the leaves stand out more clearly from the background.

8 Now build up colour on the leaves. Darken the red leaves by brushing on a very dilute mix of alizarin crimson, dropping in some green in places so that the two colours merge wet into wet. Add more cadmium yellow to the bright green mixture from Step 3 and brush it on to the central leaf, which is catching the light.

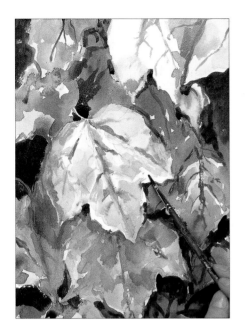

**9** Combine your basic red and green mixtures to make a very dark, almost black colour. Using a fine round brush held almost vertically, put in the very dark veins on the shaded red parts of the leaves. Mix a soft pink from titanium white and alizarin crimson and paint the pink leaf tips.

**10** Continue to build up the tones on the central leaf, which is in the most prominent position, adding more of the yellowish-green mixture from Step 8. Finally, use the dark green mixture from Step 4 to put in the veining on the central leaf, holding the brush loosely by the end of the handle to make flowing calligraphic marks.

### The finished painting

By working wet into wet, the artist has achieved some lovely, subtle colour shifts in the leaves, with pink merging into red and red into varying shades of green. The joy of painting in this way is that you can allow the paint to flow of its own accord and do a lot of the work for you. The detail of the leaf veins was added when the first washes had almost dried, so these lines are crisper without overpowering the initial washes. By holding the brush near the end of the handle, however, the artist has been able to make lovely flowing lines like those used in Chinese brush painting or calligraphy. The result is an atmospheric, spontaneous-looking study.

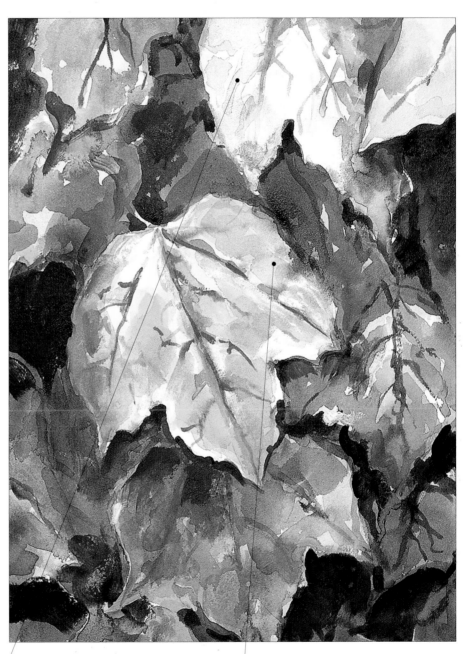

When one colour is applied on top of a colour that is almost dry, the second colour has a clearly discernible edge.

When two colours are allowed to merge wet into wet, the transition between the two is virtually imperceptible.

# Painting alla prima in oils

The term *alla prima* comes from the Italian for "at the first" and is used to describe a work (traditionally an oil painting) that is completed in a single session. No underpainting is made, and often there is no preliminary drawing. Reasonably thick, creamy paint is applied using direct and expressive brushstrokes.

Even though they are made using a relatively thick layer of paint, alla prima paintings are invariably technically accurate, as the paint dries at a similar rate over the whole image. There is no problem of an underpainting of a different consistency drying at a different rate and possibly causing the paint to crack at some point in the future.

The alla prima technique is well suited to portrait work and to landscape work done on location, as well as to preliminary studies. Size is an issue, as the work must be no larger than can be comfortably completed in a single session. To help facilitate the uniform drying of the paint, the same painting medium (preferably one that does not accelerate drying time) should be used throughout.

## Practice exercise: **Anemones painted alla prima**

Fresh spring flowers require a fresh, spontaneous approach, and painting them alla prima is a great way of capturing the delicate texture of the petals. Although the arrangement of leaves and stems looks complex, look for generalized shapes rather than trying to capture every single element. Look at the spaces between leaves, as defining these "negative shapes" will make the shapes of the leaves stand out more clearly.

### The set-up

Although this vase of flowers looks so informal that you might imagine the flowers have simply been placed there, with no thought as to their arrangement, the artist has carefully positioned them so that some flower heads are fully open while others are seen from the side. This gives the artist the opportunity to explore the structure of the blooms and makes for a more interesting picture. The colour distribution, too, is important: the reds and purples balance each other well.

### Materials
- *Canvas board*
- *B pencil*
- *Oil paints: phthalocyanine green, yellow ochre, burnt umber, cadmium yellow, titanium white, quinacridone red, ivory black, phthalocyanine blue, purple lake*
- *White spirit (paint thinner) or low-odour thinner*
- *Brushes: small flat*

1 Using a B pencil, make a careful drawing of the flowers on the canvas. Establishing the shapes of the individual elements at this stage will make it easier later on: without an underdrawing, the mass of different greens in the bottom half of the image is potentially very confusing.

2 Mix a dark green from phthalocyanine green, yellow ochre and burnt umber, thinning the mixture with just enough solvent for the paint to come off the brush easily: too much solvent will make the paint too fluid and hard to control. Using a small flat brush, begin painting the darkest leaves and the spaces between the stems.

**3** Continue adding the green leaves, using short single brush strokes to build up the forms. Lighten the mixture by adding cadmium yellow, a tiny amount of yellow ochre, and titanium white. Alternate between the two greens as you work, so that you begin to establish a sense of light and shade, and make a conscious effort to vary the angle at which you hold the brush, as this will result in marks of different thicknesses.

**4** Still using various green mixtures, gradually build up the mosaic of colour and form. Note that some of the greens are very light (achieved by adding more white to the mixture), while some are very dark (achieved by adding a little quinacridone red): work slowly and methodically, so that you do not lose track of where you are in the painting, and refer continually to your still-life set-up. Use the underdrawing only as a guide.

**5** Mix a dark red from quinacridone red, a little ivory black, cadmium yellow and yellow ochre, and start putting in the darkest reds of the anemone flowers. There are several tones of red within the same flower, so you will need to look closely to establish where the darkest reds occur. Use the same mixture for the delicate veining on the petals, using the edge of the brush to create very fine lines.

**6** While the dark red mixture is on the palette, use it to paint all the dark reds that you can see on the other flower heads. This is not only an economic use of paint, but it also forces you to work across the whole painting, rather than concentrating on one area and running the risk of overworking it.

▶

**7** Lighten the red mixture by adding titanium white and a little cadmium yellow, and begin putting in the mid tones on the anemone flowers, working around the deep reds that you have already established in the previous two steps. Use just the tip or the thin edge of the brush and apply only light pressure, as this allows you to place your strokes very precisely and paint small, delicate areas with ease.

**8** Mix a bluish-black colour from phthalocyanine blue and burnt umber and, with a few short and carefully controlled strokes, paint the dark mass that lies at the centre of each flower.

**9** Mix a yellowish green from white, a little of the original green mixture and yellow ochre and touch this colour around the dark flower centres. Mix a dark purple from purple lake and a little phthalocyanine blue and paint the darkest parts of the purple flowers, delineating the individual petals. Mix a lighter purple from quinacridone red, phthalocyanine blue and titanium white and paint the lighter purple areas.

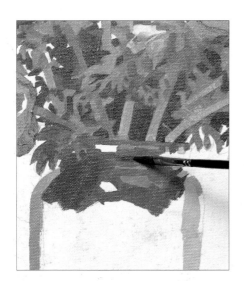

**10** Add white to the light purple mixture from the previous step and paint over the lightest areas around the centre of the purple flower. Use some of the light green mixture that you used to paint the stalks to put in the light colour on the ceramic vase, leaving the brightest highlights untouched.

**11** Add purple lake and a little burnt umber to the original dark green mixture that you used in Step 2 and paint the darker reflected colours that can be seen on both sides of the vase, taking care to paint around the highlights that you painted in Step 10. The vase is now beginning to look much more rounded and three-dimensional: the use of different tones of green helps to give it form, while the highlight shows us which direction the light is coming from and helps to enliven the composition.

**Tip**: Look carefully at the shapes of the shadows cast on the wall: although the flowers are soft, rounded shapes, some of the shadows are quite angular. Using a flat brush allows you to make precise marks: use a corner of the wedge shape to fill in detail, the end of the wedge for thin straight lines, and the full width to cover larger areas.

**12** Now paint the shadow that the flowers cast on the wall behind. Mix a purplish grey from the purple flower colour, the red mixture used in Step 7, and phthalocyanine blue. Loosely brush in the shadow, remembering to leave gaps to indicate where the light shines through the flowers on to the wall.

## The finished painting

Add lots of titanium white and a little yellow ochre to the shadow colour and put in the background. Working alla prima allows you to blend the colours on the support and capture the delicacy of the papery petals to perfection. The finished painting is a lively and realistic-looking interpretation of a loose arrangement of spring flowers.

Thin layers of paint, blended wet into wet on the support, create the delicate veining and subtle coloration of the anemone petals.

The background is painted in a single, thin layer of a pale purplish grey, using short brushstrokes of lighter paint to soften the shadow edges.

The cast shadow has the effect of throwing the vase of flowers forward.

# Glazing

A glaze is a transparent layer of paint that is applied over a layer of paint. As with traditional watercolour, light passes through the transparent glaze and is reflected back by the support or any underpainting. Glazing is a form of optical mixing as each glaze colour is separate from the next, with the mixing taking place within the eye. Each glaze needs to be dry before the next layer is applied, otherwise the colours will simply mix together as they would on the palette. Glazing techniques can be used with both oils and acrylics.

Glazed colours reflect light more readily than opaque colours, which tend to absorb light. This gives glazed works a richness and luminosity that can be lacking in paintings done using conventional mixing techniques.

Traditionally, the work began with an involved tonal underpainting in monochrome over which the colours were carefully glazed. Depending on the subject, the underpainting can be made using a warm brown, black, or even green. However, glazing techniques can also be used in conjunction with more opaque painting techniques. Glazes made over opaque layers of paint can liven up dull areas of colour, or make warm areas of colour appear cooler or cool areas warmer. This is particularly useful when painting portraits. A single colour glaze is often used over the entire picture area once it is finished and dry, which has the effect of bringing an overall harmony to the colours.

### Lightness or darkness of the glazed colour ▼
Traditionally, glazed colours were applied over a tonal underpainting. It is the tones in the monochrome underpainting that determine the lightness or darkness of the colours glazed on top.

### Physical colour mixing ▼
Physically mixing cadmium yellow (below left) and dioxazine purple (below right) creates a dull brown (bottom left). When the same two colours are glazed one over the other, the integrity of both remains intact and the result is a brighter mix in which the two colours combine optically (bottom right).

Cadmium yellow      Dioxazine purple

Physical mix      Glazed colour

### Mediums for glazes ▶
When using oil paint, which is less opaque than acrylic, use a glazing medium. With acrylic paints use a gloss painting medium; this not only thins the paint but also increases its transparency. Acrylic paints are ideal for glazing, as they dry very quickly. Certain colours, which are by their nature more transparent, are more suitable for glazing techniques than others, but even opaque colour can be used.

Oil paint straight from the tube      Oil paint plus glazing medium      Acrylic paint straight from the tube      Acrylic paint plus gloss medium

## Practice exercise: **Glass jar and chiffon**

Glazing is the ideal technique for painting transparent and semi-transparent subjects such as this tiny glass jar and chiffon scarf, as it allows colour to be built up gradually until the right density is achieved. The final effect of both transparent glass and transparent fabric is skilfully achieved Careful observation is the key, as there are many subtle shifts of tone within the scene, even though the number of colours in this particular exercise is relatively small.

Remember that you need to allow each glaze to dry completely before you apply the next one, otherwise the colours will combine in a muddy mess.

**Materials**
- *Oil paper*
- *B pencil*
- *Oil paints: phthalocyanine green, raw sienna, alizarin crimson, ultramarine blue; zinc white*
- *Thinner*
- *Drying linseed oil*
- *Brushes: medium flat, small round*

**The set-up**
Although the chiffon scarf is casually draped, it naturally falls into folds, some of which are several layers thick, and you have to assess the depth of colour very carefully. The scarf can also be seen through the glass jar, although its colour here is modified by the green of the glass.

1 Using a B pencil, make a light underdrawing, putting in the lines of the main folds in the chiffon scarf as a guide. Mix a bluish green from phthalocyanine green and a tiny amount of raw sienna. Using a medium flat brush block in the jar, leaving some areas untouched for the highlights in the glass. Indicate the cast shadow to the right of the jar.

2 Mix a pale pinkish red from alizarin crimson with a little raw sienna. Paint the scarf. Your brushstrokes should run in the same direction as the folds in the fabric; you will find that the flat brush makes it easier to paint the edges of the folds.

3 Mix a neutral grey from alizarin crimson and a little phthalocyanine green, and paint the shadow under the scarf. Mix an orangey brown from raw sienna and alizarin crimson and paint the shelf edge. Add a little phthalocyanine green and glaze it over the shelf to get some variation in colour. Use this mixture for areas where the wood can be seen through the chiffon.

▶

**4** Mix a cooler version of the scarf colour used in Step 2 by adding a tiny amount of phthalocyanine green and paint the scarf that can be seen through the jar. At this stage, simply block in the area of colour without making any attempt to work out the tones.

**5** Glaze this cooler colour over the most deeply shaded parts of the scarf. Already the scarf is beginning to take on some depth.

**6** Mix a very pale, dilute raw sienna and brush it lightly over the white background to warm up this area and make the contrast between it and the still life less stark. Using the medium flat brush, glaze alizarin crimson over the deepest-coloured parts of the scarf, where several layers of fabric overlap each other.

**7** Glaze the cool pink colour from Step 5 over the deepest folds in the fabric. Mix a dark blue-green from phthalo-cyanine green and ultramarine blue and, using a small round brush, darken the colour of the jar where necessary. Glaze this blue-green colour over some of the dark reds in the jar. Note how the two glazes modify each other: the red is cooled by the green.

**8** Continue building up the dark green colour of the jar, remembering to work around the highlights. Glaze more of the pink mixture over the most deeply coloured parts of the scarf, where several layers of fabric fall in soft folds on top of one another. Use a cooler (bluer) mix inside the jar, as the colour of the scarf in this area is affected by the green of the glass.

**9** Glaze more dark green over the jar to make a stronger contrast, so that the jar comes forwards in the scene. Reinforce the highlights in the jar with zinc white (or zinc white mixed with a tiny amount of blue-green, as appropriate).

**Tip**: Even in clear glass, highlights are rarely, if ever, pure white. Instead they are tinged with a hint of the colour of any nearby objects that are reflected in the glass. Here, the highlights are created by using a paler version of the green used for the glass jar.

## The finished painting

Thin layers of paint have been skilfully applied to build up the colours and tones. Where several layers of sheer fabric overlap one another, glazes are the perfect means of building up the colour to the right density. Each glaze modifes the preceding colour, creating optical mixes that are more lively than could be achieved by mixing colours in the palette.

Several glazes of different colours are used for the deepest-coloured areas.

One layer of thin paint is enough to portray the delicate wispy nature of the fabric.

# Scumbling

Scumbling is the technique that involves applying dry, semi-opaque paint loosely and roughly over a dry underlayer, leaving some of the underlayer visible to create optical colour mixes on the support. The technique also produces interesting surface textures in which the marks of the brush or other paint applicator may still be seen. The technique can be used with oils, acrylics, gouache, watercolour and pastels. The texture of the support plays an important part in scumbling techniques, which tend to be more successful on rough surfaces than on smooth. Having said that, however, subtle scumbling is useful for adding variation and relief to large areas of flat, uninteresting colour on smooth supports.

Scumbling is a great way of modifying colour while keeping the painted surface looking lively. For example, if an area looks too hot, you could scumble a cool colour over the top – and vice versa. Or you might choose to use the technique to paint an area of deep shadow, which is rarely if ever a uniform, flat colour; the colours thus applied will create an optical mix that looks much more lively and interesting than a physical mix of the same hues. There are lots of subjects for which scumbling is appropriate. Masses of foliage seen from a distance, clouds racing across a stormy sky, torrents of water, worn stone or distressed wood: all consist of intermingling colours and can benefit from the fresh, spontaneous look that scumbling can achieve.

Whatever medium you are using, when applying a scumble you should always work loosely and freely. If you're using a brush, scrub the paint on to the support with the brushstrokes going in different directions or even in a circular motion. A bristle or synthetic brush is best, as the fibres are hard and separate from one another; with a soft-haired watercolour brush, the fibres would stick together and detract from the irregular effect of the technique. It is best to save old, worn brushes for this technique as the scrubbing action will quickly damage the bristles of good brushes. You can also scumble paint on using a rag or sponge, or even your fingers.

**Broad scumble ▲**
Here, a stiff mix of paint is scumbled over the dry, slightly impasto paint applied previously. The paint catches on some of the brushstrokes, but in other areas the underlying layer still shows through.

**Scumbling to add interest ▲**
An area of dry, flat colour can be made more interesting by scumbling a slightly different colour over it.

**Transparent scumble using acrylics ▲**
For a more transparent scumble and delicate optical colour mixes, add acrylic medium to the paint. This increases the transparency of the paint.

**Heavily textured scumbling ▲**
For a more textured look, dot the paint on to the support straight from the tube. You can use this technique with both oils and acrylics.

**Light scumbling with a rag ▲**
To allow more of the first layer to show through, dip a rag or absorbent kitchen paper into your chosen colour and lightly touch it on to the support, so that the paint adheres only to the peaks of the brushstrokes of the first layer.

**Light colour scumbled over dark ▲**
Use a stiff, dryish mix of paint and remove some of it from the brush prior to making the mark, in the same way as you would with drybrush techniques. This allows more of the first layer to show through.

## Practice exercise: **Distressed wood and metal**

Scumbling is the perfect technique for painting weathered wood and metal, as it allows underlying colours to show through and creates interesting textures. Keep your paints fairly thick and dry, and apply the paint unevenly, so that the colour is not uniform.

Build up the scumbles gradually. If you apply too much heavy paint all at once, the subtlety of the effect will be lost. A few drops of acrylic medium improves the paint flow. In this exercise, which is painted on cardboard, the medium also acts as a size; even though the cardboard has been primed, it is still porous, and the medium prevents the paint from sinking into the surface.

### Materials
- *Cardboard primed with acrylic gesso*
- *HB pencil*
- *Acrylic paints: alizarin crimson, phthalocyanine green, raw sienna, titanium white*
- *Matt acrylic medium*
- *Brushes: large round, small round, small flat*

**The scene**
The artist came across this magnificent but rather scary-looking door knocker on a trip to Venice; small details such as this are often as evocative as views of an entire building.

1 Using an HB pencil, sketch the scene. Although the subject is small in scale, the changes in tone from one plane to another need to be carefully rendered, so make sure you put in all the detail you need. Your pencil marks will be fully covered by the paint.

2 Mix a dark, almost black, green from alizarin crimson and phthalocyanine green and add a few drops of matt acrylic medium. Using a large round brush, start painting the background.

3 Lighten the mixture for the top left of the painting, which is catching more of the light. Add some raw sienna to the mixture and brush it wet into wet into the background to get some variation in colour.

4 Mix a warm brown from raw sienna and alizarin crimson and dab it loosely over the darkest parts of the metal door knocker. This will serve as a warm base for subsequent applications of paint.

▶

5 Mix an opaque, pale metal colour from titanium white, raw sienna and a little phthalocyanine green. Using a small round brush, brush it over the lightest areas, adding more green to the mixture for those areas that are slightly cooler in tone.

6 Continue to paint the door knocker, alternating between the warm and cool mixtures used in the previous step as necessary in order to build up the form. Leave to dry.

7 Mix an opaque white from titanium white and the cool green mixture. Using a medium flat brush, loosely scumble it over the wood of the door, allowing some of the underlying colour to remain visible, creating the effect of worn, distressed paintwork.

8 Continue to scumble paint over the door, varying your mixtures by adding more green for some parts and more raw sienna for others. Remember that the light in the scene is coming from the top left, which means that the bottom right is darker and more deeply shaded.

9 The scumbling on the door establishes the mid tones of the painting, which makes it easier to assess how dark the very shaded parts need to be. Mix a dark, brownish green from raw sienna, alizarin crimson and phthalocyanine green. Using a small brush, put in the dark recesses on the face, adding more raw sienna on the right-hand side. Scumble the same colour over the round knocker.

**10** Build up the form by continuing to add shaded recesses on the face.

**11** Refine the details, using opaque mixtures of all the colours on your palette. Use a small flat brush to sharpen the outline of the door knocker with dark greens and blue-green mixes.

**Tip**: The shape of the flat brush makes it easier to give objects a crisp, sharp outline.

**The finished painting**
This painting shows just how effective scumbling can be when painting worn and weathered surfaces. Although only a limited number of colours were used, the various layers of paint imply not only the way the wooden door has been bleached by years of exposure to the sun and rain, but also create rough textures. The use of warm and cool tones of the same colours creates a convincing sense of light and shade, even though the light source itself (the sun) is not visible. This helps to build up the form of the door knocker and make it look three dimensional.

Rough scumbling adds texture to the image.

Here, the scumbling hints at the rustiness of the metal.

# Impasto

Impasto techniques involve applying and building the paint into a thick layer and are not unlike icing a cake. The word impasto is Italian for "dough" and describes the consistency of the paint used. In reality, the paint is usually more like butter; it is easy to spread and manipulate, but retains the mark of any brush or implement used to apply it. The consistency of paint straight from the tube is usually about right.

Given the amount of paint that can be used in even a modest-sized work, it can be economical to mix the paint with a medium specifically designed for impasto work. In the case of oil paint, these mediums contain drying agents that speed up the paint's drying time and cause the paint to dry at a uniform rate regardless of thickness. The medium also adds bulk to the paint without affecting its colour, so you use less paint – an important consideration given the cost of many oil paints. Acrylic paints can be bulked out using heavy gel medium and texture pastes.

By its nature, working with impasto techniques precludes the inclusion of fine detail. The work should be well planned, but painted as freely and intuitively as possible to keep it fresh. One solution is to use impasto work over an underpainting. If you are using oil paint (following the important oil-painting rule, painting "fat over lean"), use thin paint to which you have added plenty of thinner. Alternatively make the underpainting in thin acrylic paint and do the impasto work in oils.

**Using paint straight from the tube ▲**
With both oils and acrylics, you can squeeze paint straight from the tube on to the support. More often than not, artists will apply paint to the support in this way and then work into it using a painting knife or other implement.

**Using a brush ▲**
You can also squeeze the paint on to your palette and apply it with a brush. Paint from the tube is invariably of the right consistency for impasto work. Provided you do not overbrush, the brushmarks will stand proud and evident.

**Using a painting knife ▲**
You can drag and press a painting knife into thick paint and also blend colours together on the support. The marks you make will depend on the size and shape of the knife. The knife can also be used to scrape into wet paint to create textures and to remove paint that has been incorrectly positioned.

**Adding impasto medium to paint ▲**
There are a number of so-called impasto mediums, for both oils and acrylics, that can be mixed into the paint on the palette. The one shown here is a quick-drying impasto medium designed specifically for use with oils. If you are using acrylic paints, use a heavy gel medium.

**Blotting up excess oil ▲**
If your paint is too oily when you squeeze it out of the tube, it will tend to spread and flow too easily. To overcome this, simply squeeze it on to absorbent paper (a paper towel or blotting paper); the paper will absorb the oil, leaving behind a blob of thick paint.

## Practice exercise: **Pumpkins painted impasto using acrylics**

Pumpkins are highly textured vegetables: there are clear indentations on the outer surfaces delineating the different segments, while a tangled mass of fibres and hard seeds on the inside provides you with the perfect opportunity to practise impasto work. The coloration, too, gives you the chance to apply the paint thickly, dabbing on different colours to achieve the necessary variations in tone. Adding acrylic gel medium to the paint thickens it and makes it ideal for impasto work, as it holds the marks of the knife or brush. It also makes the paint go further.

### Materials
- Primed canvas
- 2B pencil
- Acrylic paints: burnt umber, cadmium red, cadmium yellow deep, phthalocyanine blue, alizarin crimson, cadmium yellow medium, yellow ochre, titanium white, sap green, cadmium orange
- Acrylic gel medium
- Brushes: small flat, medium flat
- Medium trowel-shaped painting knife

### The set-up
Arrange the pumpkins on a table or shelf, aiming for good contrasts of size: it looks more interesting if at least one vegetable is laid on its side, so that you can see the cut-off stalk. Look at the angle of the stalks, too: here, the artist has positioned the largest and the cut pumpkins with their stalks pointing towards each other, which helps to direct the viewer's eye through the picture. Cut at least one of the pumpkins open to reveal the seeds and fibres inside.

1 Using a 2B pencil, lightly sketch your composition. You do not need to put in all the detail, but indicate the striations on the largest pumpkin (these curved lines will make it easier for you to get the overall shapes right). Add the angles of the stalks, and the main internal divisions in the cut pumpkin so that you have some guidelines for when you begin to paint. When you are happy with the sketch, go over the lines in burnt umber acrylic paint, using a small flat brush. If you wish, you could underpaint the picture at this point, using watered-down acrylic paint.

2 Mix a warm dark orange from cadmium red, cadmium yellow deep, and a little burnt umber, adding acrylic gel medium to the mix to thicken it. Using the edge of the brush, paint the segments on the surface of the largest pumpkin. Mix a dark brown by adding phthalocyanine blue and alizarin crimson to the orange mixture and paint the deep shadow at the base of the pumpkin. Add cadmium yellow medium to the orange mixture to lighten it, and block in the sections, carefully painting around the stalk of the cut pumpkin.

3 Using the same dark orange mixture, outline the cut pumpkin and block in the dark area around the seeds in the middle, delineating the largest of the individual seeds in the same colour. Add yellow ochre and titanium white to the mixture and paint the fibrous area with loose, horizontal brushstrokes, varying the proportions of the mixture to create tonal variety. Add more cadmium yellow and white to the mixture and paint the pumpkin flesh around the outside of the seeded area, using a full range of brushstrokes to work around the shapes.

▶

4 Using the same mixture as in Step 2, paint the shadow between the cut pumpkin and the pumpkin on the far right. Paint the individual segments of the pumpkin on the right, then paint the cut surface in a mixture of cadmium yellow medium and titanium white. Add cadmium red to the basic warm orange mixture and block in the segments of the pumpkin.

> **Tip**: Use a hairdryer to speed up the drying time of thick acrylic paint. Once you are sure that the first layer is completely dry, you can apply further layers to build up the impasto effect without disturbing the underlying paint.

5 Mix a pale, greyish-green from titanium white, phthalocyanine blue, yellow ochre and the basic orange mix and outline the segments of the small green pumpkin on the right. Add more white to the mixture and block in the segments. Mix a pale beige for the seeds of the cut pumpkin from titanium white, yellow ochre and the pale green mixture. Use the pale beige for the top of the stalk and the pale grey-green mixture for the base of the stalk. Mix a darker green, using the grey-green mix plus orange, and paint the stalks of the two pumpkins on the far right, using the dark green for the shaded sides to create a sense of light and shade.

6 Mix a mid-tone green from sap green, yellow ochre, a little phthalocyanine blue and titanium white, and outline the segments of the green pumpkin on the bottom left of the picture. Dab the same mixture over other parts of the pumpkin too. Mix a darker green from sap green, phthalocyanine blue and alizarin crimson and paint around the first green. Brush the paint on thickly, using the side of the brush, to build up interesting textures.

7 Use the same greens to reinforce the dark lines and shadow areas on the green pumpkin on the right, which are too light in relation to the rest of the image. This also helps to create a visual link across the painting. Mix a dull brown from the dark green mixture, cadmium red, yellow ochre and white and paint the table edge, using horizontal brushstrokes to echo the direction of the wood grain. Add yellow ochre and cadmium orange to lighten the mixture, and paint the table top.

8 Add yellow ochre and titanium white to the pale brown mixture. Using a medium flat brush, paint the background, constantly varying the direction of the brushstrokes and allowing the brushstrokes to remain visible in order to enhance the impasto effect. Using the edge of a trowel-shaped painting knife, press some of the dark brown mixture on to the stalks to create a fibrous, woody texture.

**9** Dip the tip of the painting knife into the basic orange mixture and drag it over the fibrous area in the middle of the cut pumpkin to make a series of uneven lines. Add titanium white to the background colour and, using the painting knife, shape the seeds in the cut pumpkin.

## The finished painting

Using the paint thickly has allowed the artist to create a range of interesting textures that are perfectly suited to the subject – fine lines for the fibres inside the cut pumpkin, achieved through both brushwork and the use of a painting knife; splotches of thick colour on the bumpy exterior surface of the vegetables.

The fibres and seeds are created by dragging and dabbing the edge and the end of the painting knife on to the support.

Allowing the brushstrokes to remain visible creates texture and offers visual relief in an otherwise flat area.

## Practice exercise: **Impasto landscape in oils**

With its scrubby vegetation and pebbly path, this Mediterranean cliffside scene provides many opportunities for working impasto. In a landscape such as this, however, it is generally helpful to include some quieter, flatter areas, such as the sea and sky, for the viewer's eye to rest on. This exercise is painted entirely with a painting knife.

### Materials
- *Canvas-covered board primed with acrylic gesso*
- *HB pencil*
- *Oil paints: phthalocyanine blue, titanium white, ultramarine blue, alizarin crimson, cadmium lemon, sap green, burnt sienna, raw sienna*
- *Rag*
- *Small painting knife*

**The scene**

This is a classically composed scene, with the main cliff falling at the intersection of the thirds and the path leading our eye through the picture. The contrasting textures – the relative smoothness of the sea and sky versus the pebbly path and dense vegetation – make a picture that is full of interest.

**1** Using an HB pencil, lightly sketch the scene so that you have a rough guide to where to place the different elements.

**2** Mix a pale blue from phthalocyanine blue and titanium white. Using a rag, smear it across the sky. Add more phthalocyanine blue and, using a small painting knife, put in the sky, smoothing the paint out so that the coverage is fairly even.

**3** There are some deep shadows on the sea; paint these in using ultramarine blue. Still using the painting knife, apply strokes of thick titanium white for the clouds. The rough impasto work helps to give a sense of volume to the clouds.

**4** Mix a dark purplish blue from alizarin crimson and ultramarine blue and smear it over the rocky, exposed area of cliff on the right, adding some sap green to the mixture as you work down towards the path. To capture the jagged feel of the rocks, pull the paint up with the tip of the knife to form small peaks. Mix a bright green from cadmium lemon, sap green and a little burnt sienna and begin putting in the lightest parts of the foreground vegetation on the left, dabbing in a more yellow version of the mixture in parts.

**5** Mix a pale brown from raw sienna and white and paint the rough-textured ground to the right of the path.

**6** Add more raw sienna to the mixture and include some darker browns in the vegetation.

**Tip**: When painting the vegetation, angle the painting knife so that it follows the direction in which the plants naturally grow.

7 Mix a pale purple from ultramarine blue, titanium white and a little alizarin crimson and use this mixture to put in the shaded sides of the foreground rocks that lie to the right of the path. Paint the bright highlights where the sun hits the tops of the rocks in titanium white.

8 Mix a very dark green from ultramarine blue and sap green and put in the very darkest areas of the plants that are growing on the cliff side, dabbing the paint on with the tip of the painting knife. Add some alizarin crimson to the mixture and put in some slightly curved strokes, using the side of the knife, for the taller stems and branches.

9 Continue to build up textures in the vegetation and rocks, using the same colours as before. Vary the way that you apply the paint, sometimes using long thin strokes of the side of the knife and sometimes dabbing the paint on with the tip of the knife. Paint the tall, thin grass strokes on the right-hand side of the painting using a mixture of raw sienna and white.

## The finished painting

Impasto work adds great vitality to this image: you can almost reach out and feel the texture of the rocks and plants. The artist has also made full use of the range of marks that can be made with a knife, from smoothing out the sky and sea areas with the flat of the knife to dabbing on small blobs of paint with the tip, and even dragging the side of the knife over the canvas to create long, flowing marks for the thinnest stems and branches.

Thick oil and acrylic paint can be pulled up with the tip of the knife to form small peaks, as here.

Note how the knife marks echo the direction in which the plants grow.

# Removing paint

There are three main reasons for removing paint from your canvas or support: to get back to the original support, either so that you can reveal the underlying colour or so that you can paint over the area again and correct a mistake; to remove excess paint from an area that is too heavily impastoed or has become clogged with paint; and to work into paint to create textured marks.

## Removing paint to get back to the original support

If the underlying colour is very strong, it's best to try and remove it so that it doesn't affect any subsequent glazes. The method that you select depends on the medium you are using and on whether the paint is wet or dry.

### To remove wet acrylic paint ▼
Dip a rag in water and wipe it through the paint.

### To remove dried gouache paint ▼
You can remove gouache paint that has dried by brushing clean water over the paint to soften it. You can then lift off the colour with your brush or a rag and paint over the affected area again. Note that this technique cannot be used with acrylic paint as once it has dried, the paint is no longer water soluble.

## Removing excess paint

When you're doing very heavy impasto work in oils or acrylics, the canvas can become clogged with paint. If the effect is as you desire, then allow the paint to dry before applying more paint. If the effect is not what you intended, scrape off the paint and start again. Thick oil paint remains wet for weeks, so it can be scraped off the support at leisure. Thick acrylic dries in hours, so it needs to be scraped off immediately. To remove excess paint, use one of the following methods.

### Scraping off paint with a knife ▼
Hold the edge of the knife perpendicular to the support, press down firmly, and drag the knife through the wet paint to remove any surplus. This leaves a flat area of colour, in which no brush marks can be seen.

### Tonking
An alternative method is a technique known as tonking – named after the British artist Henry Tonks (1862–1937).

1 Place a sheet of newspaper over the affected area and smooth it down with your hands.

2 Peel away the paper, removing any excess paint in the process. The result is more textured than using a knife.

## Working into paint to create texture

Thick paint has a pleasing texture that comes from the marks left by the bristles of the brush. This, combined with the texture of the support, is often all that is needed. However, greater verisimilitude can often be achieved when replicating the textures present on whatever is being painted by working into the paint.

**Sgrafitto – wet paint ▲**
You can make textured marks in paint by scraping into the paint with the end of a brush. Alternatively, use a twig, the tip of a craft knife or the edge of a piece of cardboard.

**Sandpaper – dried acrylic or gouache paint ▲**
To create texture on dried acrylic and gouache paint, lightly rub sandpaper or another abrasive material over the area. Do not rub so hard that you damage the support.

## Practice exercise: **Watermelons**

Two methods of lifting off paint are used in this exercise – tonking and scraping off paint with a knife. Tonking creates some texture, whereas scraping off paint leaves a much flatter, smoother surface.

Acrylic paints are used here, although the subject and techniques that the artist employed would work equally well in oils. As acrylics dry quickly, it is a good idea to add a little retarding medium to your mixes as this gives you longer to work into the paint. Even so, it is best to work on relatively small areas – one melon at a time – finishing one off before the next.

**Materials**
- *Board primed with acrylic gesso*
- *B pencil*
- *Acrylic paints: cadmium yellow, titanium white, phthalocyanine green, olive green, alizarin crimson, cadmium red*
- *Retarding medium*
- *Small painting knife*
- *Newspaper*
- *Brushes: flat wash, medium flat, small flat*

**The scene**
The artist came across these water-melons on a market stall. Red and green are complementary colours and almost always work well together. The jagged lines of the cut melons counterbalance the rounded forms of the whole fruits.

**1** Mix a pale yellow from cadmium yellow and titanium white and, using a flat wash brush, cover the board. Leave to dry. Using a B pencil, draw the outlines of the fruits. At this stage, you don't need to put in the jagged outlines of the cut melons: an indication of the overall shape, which you can use as a guideline, is sufficient.

2 Mix a dark green from phthalo-cyanine green and olive green, adding a little retarding medium to the mixture to give yourself longer to work. Using a small painting knife, cover the first uncut watermelon with the mixture. The coverage does not have to be completely even, but try not to go outside the pencil lines.

3 Tear off a piece of newspaper and scrunch it up into a long, thin strip. Press it firmly into the paint and lift it off to reveal the toned ground underneath. Note the lovely random textures and markings that this creates: it would be much more difficult to achieve this effect by painting on the lighter colour with a brush.

4 Repeat Steps 2 and 3 until you have painted all the uncut watermelons, varying the dark greens by adding more cadmium yellow for some fruits and more olive green for others. Using a medium flat brush, fill in the spaces between the melons with a very dark green. The image immediately takes on more of a sense of depth.

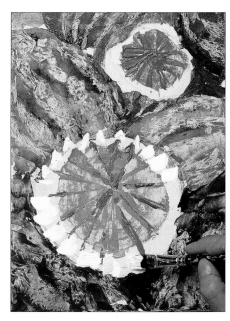

5 Mix a pinkish red from alizarin crimson, cadmium red and titanium white. Paint the red flesh of the cut melons, leaving a broad band of yellow around the edge. Place the knife tip in the centre of the melon, with the knife on its side, and scrape it clockwise, lifting off wedge-shaped areas of paint.

6 Darken the pink mixture from the previous step by adding more alizarin crimson. Dip the side of the knife into the paint and press it on to the melons to create the jagged cuts in the surface. This helps to create shading and makes the surface of the melons look three-dimensional.

7 Mix an opaque yellow from cadmium yellow and titanium white. Using a medium flat brush, paint the zigzag-shaped cut edges of the melons.

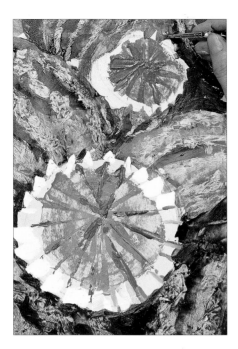

**9** Mix pale pink from alizarin crimson and titanium white and touch in the pale pinks in the melon flesh, taking the colour to the melon rim in places. Mix a pale off-white from titanium white and a little cadmium yellow and put in some thin highlight lines on the melon flesh.

**The finished painting**
This is a lively and energetic painting that uses the technique of lifting off paint to great effect to create interesting textures.

**8** Using the dark green mixture from Step 2 and a small flat brush, cut in around the edges of the melons to sharpen the shapes.

**Tip**: The dark green makes the watermelons stand out more.

**10** Mix together the dark green from Step 2 and the dark red from Step 6 to create a colour that is almost black. Paint the pips, using a small brush, and then scrape off the highlights on the pips using the end of your brush handle.

Colour has been lifted off to reveal the toned ground beneath, creating the pale stripes on the outside of the watermelons.

Scraping paint off with the side of a painting knife creates flatter, less textured areas of colour.

# Drybrush

The technique of drybrush work means precisely what it says: the brush is loaded with the minimum amount of paint and then skimmed gently over a dry surface so that it catches on the "peaks" or raised tooth of the paper or canvas, leaving part of the support showing.

It is important to splay out the bristles of the brush (or to use a fan brush) so that the individual bristle marks are evident on the support. Make sure your paint mix is not too wet: keep a rag or a piece of absorbent kitchen paper handy to blot off any excess paint, so that your brush is only very lightly loaded.

Drybrush work is a great way of conveying the texture of things like wood or weathered stone, which have a linear quality within them.

**Using a fan brush ▶**
A fan brush is ideal for drybrush work as the bristles are naturally splayed out.

**Splaying out bristles ▲**
If you do not have a fan brush, you can splay out the bristles of an ordinary brush between your finger and thumb in order to create the same kind of drybrush marks.

**Loading the brush with paint ▲**
If you simply dip your brush into your palette, there is a risk that you will overload it. To avoid this, splay out the bristles and gently pull them over a paper towel soaked in paint.

**Drybrush work over a large area ▲**
To cover a large area, dip the tip of a large bristle or household decorating brush in paint and gently drag it over the support, holding the brush at 90 degrees to the support.

## Practice exercise: **Seashells**

The delicate, linear markings and ridges on seashells such as these make them the perfect candidates for the drybrush technique. Because the shells are very light in tone, the artist decided to start from a mid-toned ground. She used button polish, which serves both to tone and to prime the ground, although you could equally well use acrylic gesso mixed with burnt umber paint.

**The set-up**
This simple still life consists of two large shells on a white background, simply lit from one side. One of the shells is placed upside down, enabling us to look inside it. Always look at your still-life subjects from different angles to find out what makes the most interesting composition.

### Materials
• *Cardboard primed with button polish*
• *HB pencil*
• *Acrylic paints: titanium white, ultramarine blue, raw sienna, cadmium red, cadmium yellow*
• *Brushes: small flat, fine round*
• *Absorbent kitchen paper*

1 Sketch the shells with an HB pencil. Paint the background in a dilute wash of white and ultramarine. Paint the shadows in a purplish grey mixed from ultramarine and raw sienna. Mix a warm-toned mix of white and raw sienna and a cool-toned mix of white and ultramarine. Alternating between them, begin painting the shells.

2 Mix a purplish colour from cadmium red and ultramarine blue. Load the paintbrush, dab off any excess paint on a piece of kitchen paper, and paint the dark colour on the inside of the left-hand shell. Add white to the mixture to make it more opaque and put in the dark markings on the other shell. Using a fine round brush and the warm-toned mixture from Step 1, drybrush the grooves on the shell.

3 Mix a dark purple from cadmium red and ultramarine blue and drybrush on the markings on the interior of the left-hand shell. Add a tiny amount of raw sienna to the cool-toned mixture from Step 1 and put in the slightly shaded areas of the right-hand shell, making sure your brushstrokes follow the direction of the grooves on the shells to reinforce the three-dimensional impression.

4 Mix a very pale yellow from cadmium yellow and titanium white and paint the tops of the ridges on the right-hand shell. Continue putting in the dark patterning on the shells, using the drybrush technique all the time to create texture and imitate the rough, irregular markings on the shells.

5 Mix a mid-toned grey from titanium white, cadmium yellow and raw sienna. Scumble the mixture over the background, carefully brushing around the shadows. Using the purple mixture from Step 3, reinforce the lines in the left-hand shell.

## The finished painting

These shells have a jagged and irregular surface. Drybrush work is the perfect way to paint the small, spiny ridges. As the brushes are skimmed only lightly over the surface of the support, the technique also allows underlying colours to show through, conveying the mottled, irregular coloration of the shells very effectively. The key with any isubject like this is not to overwork it and lose the spontaneity of the image.

6 Reinforce the dark patterning on the shells where necessary, using the same colours as before.

Drybrush work captures these small ridges to perfection.

# Gouache techniques

The techniques that are used when painting in gouache are very similar to those used when working in watercolour, and these two pages give a brief summary of the most common methods. Like watercolour, gouache is water soluble – but unlike watercolour (which is transparent), gouache is opaque. This means that, because of its opacity, light pale colours can be painted over dark colours, just as one would when using certain oil or acrylic techniques. However, gouache paint can also be heavily diluted with water and used in semi-transparent washes, as one would use watercolour paint. It is common practice to combine the two approaches in the same work.

## Wet on dry

Paint applied to a dry surface creates marks that retain their edge and shape, and the paint tends to stay where it is put. However, the underlying support or paint layer must be completely dry before you apply a second layer, or else the effect will be lost. As gouache can easily be made re-soluble when it is re-wet, wet colour needs to be applied over a dry colour using quick, sure brushstrokes in order not to pick up any of the underlying colour.

### Wet paint applied to dry paper ▼
Below, the first (red) wash was allowed to dry completely before strokes of yellow paint were applied on top. The yellow has not spread at all, but retained its original edges. As gouache is opaque, of course, it is possible to apply a light colour on top of a dark one without the underlying colour showing through – unlike watercolour.

## Wet into wet

Paint applied to a surface that is already wet with paint or water will bleed and spread, creating a soft, seductive blend of colour. The technique takes practice to control, as the results can, to a certain extent, be unpredictable. The extent and speed of the paint spread depends on the wetness of the surface. On a damp surface, paint will spread slowly, within a contained area. On a visibly wet surface, paint will spread rapidly and not always in a predicted direction. However, you can control the direction in which the paint spreads by tilting the support.

## Masking

Masking is done to prevent paint from getting on to unwanted areas or to create an edge that would be impossible using any other method. Masking fluid can be used with thin washes, although heavy, thick paint can prevent the dry fluid from being removed. Masking tape and film (frisket paper) can be used to create straight edges or cut to create curved edges. Torn paper can be used in the same way as tape, while torn fabric with frayed edges can create wonderful effects.

### Different types of mask ▼
Masking fluid and thin strips of torn and untorn masking tape were applied to the unpainted paper before a wash of orange paint was brushed over the whole area. When the paint was dry the masks were removed, revealing the unpainted paper underneath.

### Wet paint applied to damp paper ▼
Applied over a slightly damp first layer, the red paint has spread a little.

## Resist techniques

Wax candle or wax crayon can be used to draw on to the dry support or dry paint work. When the area is painted over, the wax will repel the watery paint, which will only settle in areas where there is no wax. If the paint is too thick it will settle on the wax and the effect will be lost. The exact result depends on how much pressure you apply and on the type of surface on which you are working: the wax will leave more broken marks on a rough surface than on a smooth one. Resists are a useful technique for painting waves or turbulent water, trackways and ploughed fields.

### Candle wax ▼
Here, a candle was rubbed over parts of the unpainted paper before a wash of green paint was applied. The wax repels the water in the paint, leaving a textured effect.

## Spattering

Gouache paint can be spattered on to a dry or a wet surface: blobs of paint spattered on to a dry surface will retain their shape, while blobs spattered on to a wet surface will soften and spread. Very wet paint tends to make larger blobs, as more paint is picked up by the brush and leaves it easily when the brush is tapped. Thick paint clings to the brush and is reluctant to leave it when tapped, resulting in a fine spatter. The distance that you hold the brush from the support also has an effect on the spatter density and size. It is hard to control exactly where spatters will go, and you may need to mask certain areas of your painting to prevent blobs of paint accidentally falling on them. Spattering is a useful technique for painting pebbles or gravel paths.

### Spatter texture ▼
Paint can be spattered by tapping your finger against the handle of a brush loaded with paint or by pulling back the bristles of the brush with your fingertips to release a fine spray. Many artists keep old toothbrushes to use for spattering.

## Sgrafitto

The technique of scratching into paint is known as sgrafitto. It is used to create texture and highlights. You can scratch or scrape into dry paint to reveal previously applied paint or the surface of the support. Any sharp implement can be used, as can abrasives such as sandpaper. Once made, the scratch marks can be left as they are or worked over using more paint. Sgrafitto can also be used to remove areas of paint to correct mistakes, although the technique is less successful if so-called staining colours have been used, as they tend to soak into the support and stain the paper fibres to a greater depth than non-staining colours. Sgrafitto techniques are best used on heavy or thick supports as there is less risk of cutting through the paper.

### Sandpaper and craft (utility) knife ▼
On the left, fine sandpaper was rubbed over a wash of dry paint – a useful technique for creating texture on rock faces or areas of grassland. On the right, paint was scratched off using the tip of a knife – good for highlights such as sun touching water.

## Sponging

Both natural and man-made sponges can be dipped into paint and used to create textural effects and apply washes of colour. Natural sponges tend to have a more random texture than man-made sponges and leave a more pleasing mark. Various shapes and sizes are available, and sponges can be cut or pulled apart for work on small areas. Thin mixes of gouache tend to soak into the sponge, so you will need to mix up a large quantity of paint. Thick paint, however, tends to be picked up only on the sponge surface. Complex textural marks can be made by building up a sequence of sponge marks in layers, allowing each one to dry before you apply the next. You can also dip sponges in water and wipe them over the paper surface to remove paint.

### Natural sponge ▼
Here you can see the effect of pressing a sponge loaded with paint several times over the same area: the paint is quite dense, but the pattern is sufficiently broken to create a textured effect that is useful for painting things like distant areas of foliage.

## Drybrush

Any type of brush can be used to apply drybrush marks, but fan brushes intended for blending oil or acrylic paint are particularly effective. If you do not have a fan brush, you can create the same effect by loading a brush with paint and then splaying out the bristles with your fingers before applying the brush to the support. The technique can be slow, but if it is applied with care and patience it is possible to build a beautiful textured surface. Paint needs to be used sparingly or the effect will be lost. Drybrush is a useful technique for painting the flow and fall of fabric, birds' feathers and animal fur.

### Drybrush marks with splayed-out brush ▶
This technique creates the effect of regularly spaced lines, with areas of the support showing through the paint.

## Practice exercise: **Combining gouache techniques**

This simple still life gives you the chance to practise different gouache techniques within the same painting: overlaying colours; wet into wet and wet on dry; various ways of creating textures, including spattering and sponging; and exploiting the natural chalky consistency and opacity of gouache paint.

The artist chose watercolour board as the support for this painting, as it has a smooth surface that is ideal for capturing fine detail.

Crabs and other shellfish, such as lobsters, langoustines and mussels, make fascinating subjects for still lifes as their shells contain many variations in colour, providing you with the ideal opportunity to practise assessing different tones.

In this project the darkest colours are put down first – unlike pure transparent watercolour, where you have to work from light to dark. Establishing the dark colours first gives you a strong guide to follow for placing the individual elements of the scene. It also keeps the colours looking fresh and lively: light gouache colours contain proportionally higher amounts of chalk, which means that any colours that are put down on top of them may pick up some of the chalk and lose their clarity. Dark gouache colours, on the other hand, contain very little chalk, so any light colours that are put down on top of them will not pick up the chalk. Nonetheless, the chalk content of the paint also makes it ideal for this particular subject as it allows you to recreate the slightly matt surface of the crab shell.

### Materials
- *Watercolour board*
- *HB pencil*
- *Gouache paints: cadmium red deep, lamp black, raw sienna, phthalocyanine blue, cadmium red medium, cadmium yellow lemon, yellow ochre, cadmium yellow light, zinc white*
- *Brushes: fine round, medium round*
- *Cardboard*
- *Pencil: red*

### The set-up
In terms of both its size and its colour the crab dominates the composition. The red-and-white tablecloth and napkin echo the coloration of both the crab shell and the plate on which it is set; they also offer a contrast of texture. The lemons, with their slightly pitted outer skin, provide an interesting contrast of texture and colour.

1 Using an HB pencil, make an underdrawing of your still-life set-up. It is easy to lose track of where you are in a painting like this, so make sure you put down all the information you are likely to need. The segments of the crab claws, the indentations on the shell, and the lines of the draped napkin are all useful guidelines.

2 Mix a dark reddish brown from cadmium red deep, lamp black and raw sienna. Using a fine round brush, paint the darkest red of the crab shell and claws. Add a little more lamp black and some phthalocyanine blue to the mixture and paint the very dark tips of the claws. Mix lamp black and phthalocyanine blue together and paint the border of the plate. Leave to dry.

3 Mix a dark, brownish red from raw sienna and cadmium red medium. Using a fine round brush put in the next darkest parts of the crab claws, taking care to follow the hard-edged, angular shape of the segments. Switch to a medium round brush and begin to apply the same colour to the body of the crab, using the side of the brush to scrub on the colour.

5 Add more cadmium red deep and a little yellow ochre to the brownish red mixture from step 3 and paint more of the crab shell and claws. This is a slightly lighter and redder tone than the ones used to date; with the transition from dark tones to mid-tones, the three-dimensional form of the crab is becoming more evident.

4 Spatter some of the brownish red mixture from Step 3 over the body of the crab and leave to dry. While you are waiting for the brown paint to dry, brush cadmium yellow lemon over the lemons in order to establish the base colour. Leave to dry.

▶

**6** Add cadmium yellow light to the mixture to make it more orange and paint the lighter tones around the end of the shell and claws. Now start to put in some colour on the red-and-white napkin on the right. Although it looks predominantly white, the white is not as bright and pure as the brightest areas on the plate, so mix a pale, yellow-tinged grey from yellow ochre, zinc white and a little lamp black. Using a medium round brush, brush the mixture over the napkin to establish the underlying colour. Leave to dry.

**7** Add some cadmium red deep to the orange mixture from the previous step and lightly dot it over the crab's shell. Leave to dry.

**Tip**: Study the crab shell carefully before you apply the paint. The indented areas are slightly darker in tone, and this helps you to convey the gently undulating nature of the hard shell.

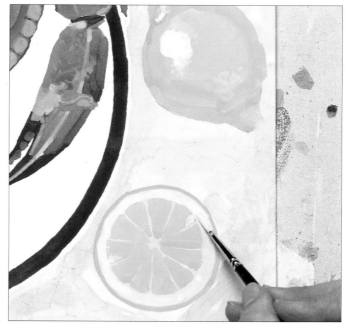

**8** Mix a very pale yellow from yellow ochre and white and, using a fine brush, paint the bright highlights on the shell – around the scalloped edge, for example. Mix a pale and dilute reddish orange from cadmium red medium and cadmium yellow light. Dip a clean sponge into the mixture and dab it over the shell to build up tone and texture. Leave to dry. You may want to repeat the sponging to build up more texture, but do not make any decision on this until you've seen how the first application looks.

**9** Mix a warm yellow from cadmium yellow lemon and a tiny amount of cadmium red medium and paint the lemon in mid-tones, leaving some of the underlying colour as the highlight, the outer rim of the cut lemon, and the segments of the cut lemon, with spaces between the segments. Paint the pith of the cut lemon in a mixture of cadmium yellow lemon and zinc white. Mix a greener yellow from cadmium yellow lemon with a little phthalocyanine blue and paint the shaded underside of the whole lemon.

**10** Continue building up texture on the shell, using the same mixtures as before. To create more tonal variation, dip a brush in clean water and scrub over any areas that you judge to be too dark, in order to soften the paint; you can then either lift off some of the paint, rinsing your brush periodically as you do so, or re-blend it.

**11** Using the same grey as before, block in the shadow areas on the napkin. Leave to dry. The cloth is now starting to look three-dimensional, as the folds in the cloth gradually take shape.

**12** Mix a cool grey from phthalocyanine blue, lamp black and white and, using a medium round brush, paint the shadows cast on the white plate by the crab's body. Use the same colour to paint the shadow cast by the plate itself.

**Tip**: Most people seem to find it easier to paint straight vertical lines than horizontal ones, so turn the painting around to paint the horizontal lines.

**13** Add lots of zinc white to the shadow mixture to make a very pale grey and paint the remainder of the white plate, leaving a few of the very brightest highlight areas untouched. Using a fine brush, paint the vertical red lines of the red-and-white cloth on which the plate sits; you may find it easiest to rest your painting hand on your other hand or on a straightedge to steady it. Leave to dry, then paint the horizontal lines.

▶

**14** Dip the edge of a piece of cardboard in white paint and press it on to the support to create the highlights on the napkin, scraping and dragging it over the surface like a flat brush and "painting" around the shadows. This allows you to create sharp edges that would be harder to achieve with a brush.

**15** Draw thin red lines on the napkin with a red pencil, noting how the lines change direction with the folds in the cloth. The pencil marks are softer and thinner than you could achieve with a brush, which ensures that this area does not compete for attention with either the crab or the red-and-white cloth on the left of the image.

**16** Using a fine round brush, stipple cadmium yellow light over the surface of the whole lemon to create the pitted texture of the skin.

**17** Mix a dark reddish brown from cadmium red, phthalocyanine blue and raw sienna and stipple it on to the crab claws for extra texture.

## The finished painting

This is a richly textured still life that demonstrates the versatility of gouache. Although the composition is simple, it has been handled with skill. The colours are well balanced, with the red of the cloths echoing the tones in the crab shell and the white of the plate and cloths and the bright yellow of the lemons offsetting the deeper tones used elsewhere.

The brightest highlight areas on the plate are left unpainted.

Spattering, sponging and wet-into-wet applications of paint combine to create a range of lively textures on the crab shell.

The chalky, opaque nature of gouache paint is ideally suited to painting the pith of the lemon.

# Index